AS/A-LEVEL YEAR 1

STUDENT GUIDE

Ps

Psych
appro
biopsy

Molly Marshall

PHILIP ALLAN FOR
HODDER
EDUCATION
AN HACHETTE UK COMPANY

Philip Allan, an imprint of Hodder Education, an Hachette UK company, Blenheim Court, George Street, Banbury, Oxfordshire OX16 5BH

Orders

Bookpoint Ltd, 130 Milton Park, Abingdon, Oxfordshire OX14 4SB

tel: 01235 827827

fax: 01235 400401

e-mail: education@bookpoint.co.uk

Lines are open 9.00 a.m.–5.00 p.m., Monday to Saturday, with a 24-hour message answering service. You can also order through the Hodder Education website: www.hoddereducation.co.uk

© Molly Marshall 2015

ISBN 978-1-4718-4381-5

First printed 2015

Impression number 5 4 3 2 1

Year 2018 2017 2016 2015

This guide has been written specifically to support students preparing for the AQA AS and A-level Psychology examinations. The content has been neither approved nor endorsed by AQA and remains the sole responsibility of the author.

Typeset by Integra Software Services Pvt. Ltd., Pondicherry, India

Cover photo: Shutter81/Fotolia

Printed in Italy

Hachette UK's policy is to use papers that are natural, renewable and recyclable products and made from wood grown in sustainable forests. The logging and manufacturing processes are expected to conform to the environmental regulations of the country of origin.

Contents

Content Guidance

AS *and* A-level: Origins of psychology: Wilhelm Wundt • Learning approaches • The cognitive approach • The biological approach

A-level *only*: The psychodynamic approach • Humanistic psychology • Comparison of approaches

AS *and* A-level: Approaches to psychology: a glossary of terms

AS *and* A-level: The divisions of the nervous system • The structure and function of sensory, relay and motor neurons • The function of the endocrine system • The fight or flight response

A-level *only*: Localisation of function in the brain • Ways of studying the brain • Biological rhythms

AS *and* A-level: Biopsychology: glossary of terms

AS *and* A-level: Experimental method • Observational techniques. • Self-report techniques • Correlations

A-level *only*: Case studies • Content analysis

AS *and* A-level: Ethics • Aims and hypotheses • Sampling • Pilot studies • Experimental designs • Observational design • Questionnaire construction • Variables and control • Demand characteristics and investigator effects • The role of peer review in the scientific process

A-level *only*: Reliability and types of validity • Features of science • Reporting psychological investigations

AS *and* A-level: Quantitative and qualitative data • Primary and secondary data • Descriptive statistics • Presentation and display of quantitative data • Distributions and correlation

A-level *only*: Levels of measurement • Content analysis and coding

Questions & Answers

■Getting the most from this book

Exam-style questions

Commentary on the questions

Tips on what you need to do to gain full marks, indicated by the icon **e**

Sample student answers

Practise the questions, then look at the student answers that follow.

Commentary on sample student answers

Find out how many marks each answer would be awarded in the exam and then read the comments (preceded by the icon **e**) following each student answer. Annotations that link back to points made in the student answers show exactly how and where marks are gained or lost.

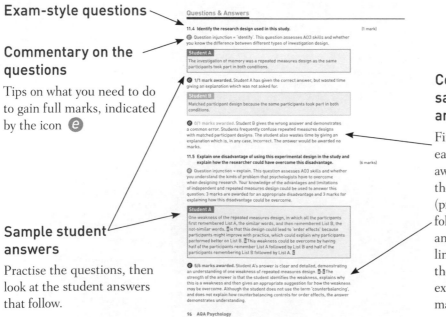

■ About this book

This is a guide to **approaches in psychology**, **biopsychology** and **research methods,** including **data handling and analysis** and **inferential testing**, which are examined on AS and A-level Paper 2. The guide is intended as a revision aid rather than as a textbook or revision guide.

For each of the topics — approaches in psychology, biopsychology and research methods — the following are provided:

- appropriate content relevant to each topic. This is not intended as the *only* appropriate content for a given topic, but gives you an idea of what you might include and how you might present an answer to a question on a particular aspect of the specification
- a glossary of key terms, constructed to be succinct but informative
- example questions in the style of AQA examination questions, together with full explanations of their requirements as well as the appropriate breakdown of marks between AO1, AO2 and AO3 skills
- an example of an A/B-grade response to each of these questions, showing how the question might be answered by a strong student
- an example of a C/D-grade response to each of these questions, with comments showing where marks have been gained or lost

Note that some aspects of topics are only examined at A-level, not AS. Where this is the case the following note appears after the relevant heading:

'This topic is not examined at AS.'

This is also made clear on the Contents page.

NB Psychopathology, which is also examined on AS Paper 2, is covered in the Student Guide *AQA Psychology: Introductory topics in psychology (includes psychopathology)* which is also published by Philip Allan for Hodder Education (ISBN 978-1-4718-4372-3).

How to use this guide

This guide is not intended to provide a set of model answers to possible examination questions, or an account of the right material to include in any examination question. It is intended to give you an idea of how your examination will be structured and how you might improve your examination performance.

You should read through the relevant topic in the Content Guidance section before you attempt a question from the Questions & Answers section. Look at the sample answers only after you have tackled the question yourself.

Content Guidance

This section gives content guidance on the topics of approaches in psychology, biopsychology and research methods, including data handling and analysis and inferential testing. It is important to note that this guide can be used by both AS and A-level students as the topics (and part topics) that are assessed at AS and A-level are clearly identified.

Each topic contains information on the theories and studies that comprise the unit content. Knowledge of appropriate theories, studies and research methods is essential for the examination. It is also important to be able to assess the value of these theories, studies and research methods.

At the end of each topic a glossary of key terms is provided — those terms that you will need to use, or may be asked to define, in an examination. Author names and publication dates have been given when referring to research studies. The full references for these studies should be available in textbooks should you wish to read about or research the topic further.

■ Approaches in psychology

Origins of psychology: Wilhelm Wundt

Wundt opened the Institute for Experimental Psychology in Germany in 1879. This marked the beginning of modern psychology. Wundt's aim was to record thoughts and sensations, and, in order to reveal their underlying structure, to analyse them into their constituent elements, in much the same way as chemists or physicists do. He wanted to study the structure of the human mind and concentrated on three areas of mental functioning: thoughts, images and feelings. Today, these areas are studied in cognitive psychology.

Wundt showed that psychology could be a valid experimental science. He believed in reductionism — that consciousness could be broken down (or reduced) to its basic elements without sacrificing any of the properties of the whole. Wundt argued that conscious mental states could be scientifically studied using introspection. **Introspection** is the examination of one's own conscious thoughts and feelings. Wundt's method of introspection did not remain a fundamental tool of psychological experiments beyond the early 1920s. However, his greatest contribution was to show that psychology could be a valid experimental science — in effect, he was the first psychologist.

Learning approaches

The behaviourist approach

The behaviourist approach makes **three assumptions**. First, it assumes that all behaviour is learned; second, that what has been learned can be unlearned; and third, that abnormal behaviour is learned in the same way as normal behaviour.

Behaviourists propose that **classical conditioning** can explain phobias. In classical conditioning, an unconditioned stimulus, such as an unexpected loud noise, triggers a natural reflex, e.g. the startle response and fear. But, if another stimulus, e.g. seeing a spider, occurs at the same time, this may in future elicit the fear response. Watson and Rayner (1920) demonstrated how classical conditioning could explain the way in which fear could be learned.

Behaviourists also propose that behaviour can be learned by the process of **operant conditioning**, in which behaviour is learned through the consequences of our actions.

Behaviourism developed out of dissatisfaction with the psychodynamic approach and earlier theories of consciousness. Psychodynamic methods rely on introspection and subjective interpretation and are based on hypothetical constructs and non-testable or unscientific ideas.

John Watson wanted a theory of behaviour that was testable. Watson built his theory on the work of Pavlov and Thorndike. Pavlov's work on the digestive system of dogs in the late nineteenth century had given rise to classical conditioning. Thorndike's work on observation of learning in various species had led to his 'law of effect'. He claimed that animals learn by trial and error and that a successful outcome (reinforcement) will result in that behaviour being repeated whereas a negative outcome (punishment) will result in that behaviour becoming extinct. This formed the basis of Skinner's work on operant conditioning.

Behaviourists believe that we are a product of our environment, that at birth we are a 'tabula rasa' or blank slate. Our genetic make-up is largely ignored and our personality, IQ, achievements and behaviour are shaped by the environment in which we are reared. Behaviourism is at the extreme end of nurture in the nature–nurture debate.

Classical conditioning

Pavlov noticed that his dogs would start to salivate when they heard the footsteps of the research assistant who was going to feed them. He realised that the dogs had learned to associate food with the footsteps and wondered if this association would extend to other things, most famously the ringing of a bell.

In classical conditioning a neutral stimulus (e.g. bell) is paired with an unconditioned stimulus (UCS) (e.g. food) and this is followed by an unconditioned response (UCR). Once the neutral stimulus is associated with the UCS, it changes to being a conditioned stimulus (CS) and the response becomes a conditioned response (CR).

Classical conditioning is simply the association of two events that occur together (e.g. bell and food, rat and loud noise), which then results in a response being transferred from one to the other (e.g. bell elicits salivation). In classical conditioning, the behavioural response is one we are not able to control — it is reflex behaviour.

Knowledge check 1

Outline the assumptions of the behaviourist approach.

Key study: Watson and Rayner (1920)

Little Albert

Aims: To find out whether they could classically condition fear of an animal by simultaneously presenting the animal and banging a steel bar so that the loud noise would frighten the child.

Participant: 'Albert B' aged 9 months. The infant was healthy, well-developed and unemotional. Before the experiment, Albert was given baseline emotional tests. The infant was then exposed, briefly and for the first time, to a white rat, a rabbit, a dog, a monkey etc. During these tests, Little Albert showed no fear toward any of these. The experimenters also banged a hammer against a suspended steel bar to make a loud noise. Albert reacted fearfully, he trembled and he suddenly began crying.

Procedure: The experiment began when Albert was just over 11 months old. Albert was placed on a mattress on a table in the middle of a room. A white rat was placed near Albert and he was allowed to play with it. At this point, the child showed no fear of the rat and played with it. In later trials, Watson and Rayner struck a suspended steel bar with a hammer behind Albert's back when the baby touched the rat. As he heard the noise Little Albert cried and showed fear. After seven such pairings of the two stimuli, Albert was presented with only the rat. He became very distressed as the rat appeared in the room. He cried, turned away from the rat, and tried to move away. 17 days after the original pairing of the stimuli, Watson took a non-white rabbit into the room and Albert became distressed. After 31 days of the experiment, Albert was taken from the hospital by his mother.

Conclusions: Watson and Rayner concluded that they had succeeded in conditioning in an infant fear of an animal that the child would not ordinarily be frightened of. Stimulus generalisation was also claimed in that Albert transferred the fear to other similar stimuli.

> **Knowledge check 2**
>
> Identify the neutral stimulus and the unconditioned stimulus in the Watson and Raynor experiment.

Operant conditioning

Edward Thorndike founded this form of learning when in 1911 he described his 'law of effect.' He reported that a behaviour followed by favourable consequences would cause the behaviour to be repeated whereas one followed by negative consequences would result in the behaviour being less likely in future.

Operant conditioning suggests that consequences of behaviour, punishment or reward, determine whether that behaviour will be repeated. 'Operant' since the animal/person operates on the environment and then faces the consequences, whether positive or negative.

Skinner believed that the best way to understand behaviour is to look at the causes of an action and its consequences. He called this approach operant conditioning. He studied operant conditioning by conducting experiments using animals which he placed in a 'Skinner box'. Operant conditioning means changing behaviour by the use of reinforcement which is given after the desired response. Skinner identified three types of response or operant that can follow behaviour:

- Neutral operants: responses from the environment that neither increase nor decrease the probability of a behaviour being repeated.
- Reinforcers: responses from the environment that increase the probability of a behaviour being repeated. Reinforcers can be either positive or negative.
- Punishers: responses from the environment that decrease the likelihood of a behaviour being repeated. Punishment weakens behaviour.

Skinner showed how **positive reinforcement** worked by placing a hungry rat in his Skinner box. The box contained a lever in the side and as the rat moved about the box it would accidentally knock the lever and a food pellet would drop into a container next to the lever. The rats quickly learned to go straight to the lever after a few times of being put in the box because if they pressed the lever the consequence was receiving food — this ensured that they would repeat the action again and again. Positive reinforcement strengthens a behaviour by providing a consequence an individual finds rewarding.

The removal of something unpleasant can also strengthen behaviour. This is known as **negative reinforcement** because it is the removal of an adverse stimulus which is 'rewarding' to the animal. Negative reinforcement strengthens behaviour because it stops or removes an unpleasant experience. Skinner showed how negative reinforcement worked by placing a rat in his Skinner box and then subjecting it to an unpleasant electric shock. As the rat moved about the box it would accidentally knock the lever and the electric current would be switched off. The rats quickly learned to go straight to the lever after a few times of being put in the box. The consequence of escaping the electric shock ensured that they would repeat the action again and again.

> **Knowledge check 3**
>
> What is the difference between positive and negative reinforcement?

Social learning theory

In social learning theory Albert Bandura (1977) states that behaviour is learned from the environment through the process of observational learning.

Bandura proposes that humans are active information processors who think about the relationship between their behaviour and its consequences. Observational learning could not occur unless cognitive processes were at work. Children observe the people around them and the people who are observed are called models. Children are surrounded by many influential models, such as parents, characters on television, friends within their peer group and teachers at school. These models provide examples of behaviour to observe and imitate (e.g. masculine and feminine, pro and anti-social etc.)

Children pay attention to some of these models and at a later date they may imitate the behaviour they have observed. A child is more likely to attend to and imitate models it perceives as similar to him- or herself and thus is more likely to imitate behaviour modelled by people of the same sex. Others will respond to the behaviour the child imitates with either reinforcement or punishment. If a child imitates a model's behaviour and the consequences are rewarding, the child is likely to continue performing the behaviour. Bandura also found that a child will also take into account what happens to 'the model' when deciding whether or not to copy someone's actions. This is known as **vicarious reinforcement**.

Bandura also proposes that children will choose 'role models' with whom they identify. These may be people they know, such as parents or siblings, or fantasy characters or people in the media. The child identifies with a role model because the model has a quality which the child would like to possess. **Identification** occurs with the model and involves adopting the observed behaviours, values, beliefs and attitudes of the person. Identification may involve a number of behaviours being adopted whereas imitation usually involves copying a single behaviour.

The term identification as used by social learning theory is similar to the Freudian term related to the Oedipus complex. For example, they both involve internalising or adopting another person's behaviour. However, during the Oedipus complex the child can only identify with the same-sex parent, whereas with social learning theory the person (child or adult) can potentially identify with any other person.

Key study: Bandura et al. (1961)

Aim: To find out whether aggression can be learned through imitation. The study focused on both imitation of aggression generally and the importance of gender — it was thought that children were more likely to imitate a same-sex model.

Procedures: Participants were children from a university nursery school (Stanford): 36 boys and 36 girls aged between 37 and 69 months (approximately 3 to 5 years). The mean age was 52 months (about 4½ years). There were two adult 'models', a male and a female, plus a female experimenter.

Phase 1: the model (exposure to aggression)

Each child was taken on his or her own to a room where there were lots of toys including, in one corner, a 5-foot inflatable Bobo doll and a mallet. The experimenter invited the 'model' to join them and then left the room for about 10 minutes.

There were three conditions (with 24 children in each):
- **Non-aggressive condition:** the model played with the toys in a quiet manner.
- **Aggressive condition:** the model spent the first minute playing quietly but then turned to the Bobo doll and spent the rest of the time being aggressive towards it. This included specific acts which might later be imitated, namely laying the doll on its side, sitting on it and repeatedly punching it on the nose. Then picking the doll up and striking it on the head with the mallet, throwing the doll in the air and kicking it about the room. This was done three times accompanied by various comments such as 'POW' and 'He sure is a tough fellow'.
- **Control:** the report does not say what treatment these children received.

In order to ensure that each group contained equally aggressive children, observations were done of the children beforehand by an experimenter who knew the children well and one of the children's teachers. They rated the children, using a 5-point scale, in terms of their physical aggression, verbal aggression, aggression towards inanimate objects and 'aggressive inhibition' (the extent to which a child resisted being aggressive when provoked). Each child had 4 marks which were then added together to give an aggression score.

→

Phase 2: tests for imitation

The children were taken to another room to see whether they would imitate the model's behaviour, and thus show evidence of learning a new behaviour and/or increased aggressiveness.

In order to find this out, it was necessary to 'mildly' provoke the children to behave aggressively. This was especially necessary for the children in the non-aggressive condition who would otherwise have no reason to behave aggressively. The provocation was achieved by showing the children a room of attractive toys and then saying they could not play with these.

The children were moved to another room which contained some aggressive toys (e.g. a mallet, and a dart gun), some non-aggressive toys (e.g. dolls and farm animals) and a 3-foot Bobo doll.

The experimenter stayed with the child while he or she played for 20 minutes, during which time the child was observed through a one-way mirror by the male model and, some of the time, another observer. The observers recorded what the child was doing every 5 seconds, using the following measures:

- **Imitation of physical aggression:** any specific acts which were imitated.
- **Imitative verbal aggression:** any phrases which were imitated, such as 'POW'.
- **Imitative non-aggressive verbal responses:** such as 'He keeps coming back for more'.
- **Non-imitative physical and verbal aggression:** aggressive acts directed at toys other than Bobo, for example saying things not said by the model, or playing with the gun.

Findings: children imitated the models they saw both in terms of specific acts and in general levels of their behaviour.

- **Imitation.** Children in the aggressive condition imitated many of the model's physical and verbal behaviours, both aggressive and non-aggressive. Children in the non-aggressive condition displayed very few of these behaviours — 70% of them had zero scores.
- **Non-imitative aggression.** The aggressive group displayed much more non-imitative aggression than the non-aggressive group.
- **Non-aggressive behaviour.** Children in the non-aggression condition spent more time playing non-aggressively with dolls than children in the other groups, and also spent more time just sitting and playing with nothing.
- **Gender.** Boys imitated more physical aggression than girls but not verbal aggression. The was some evidence of a 'same-sex effect' between model and children, in other words, boys were more aggressive if they watched a male rather than a female model and girls were more affected by a female model.

Interpretation: Bandura concluded that learning can take place in the absence of either classical or operant conditioning. The children imitated the model's behaviour in the *absence* of any rewards.

Exam tip

You could be asked to explain the difference between classical and operant conditioning.

Evaluation

Strengths

- The behaviourist approach proposes a simple testable explanation that is supported by experimental evidence.
- The behaviourist approach is hopeful as it predicts that people can change (re-learn) their behaviour.

Limitations

- The approach is criticised as being dehumanising and mechanistic (Heather 1976). People are reduced to programmed stimulus–response units.
- The approach cannot explain all psychological disorders. Conditioning cannot cure disorders, e.g. schizophrenia.

The cognitive approach

Cognitive psychologists believe that to understand human behaviour we must understand the internal processes of the human mind. The cognitive approach is based on the assumption that the human mind is like an information processor and that people have the free will to control how they select, store and think about information.

The cognitive approach had become the dominant approach in psychology by the late 1970s and the arrival of the computer gave cognitive psychology the terminology and metaphor it needed to investigate the human mind. The cognitive approach uses computer analogies to explain the workings of the human mind and adopts an information processing approach — sensory input, some sort of process, and behavioural output — comparing mental functions to the latest developments in computer hardware. Cognitive psychologists study internal processes including perception, attention, language, memory and thinking. Cognitive psychologists usually use laboratory experiments to study behaviour because the cognitive approach is a scientific one. For example, participants will take part in memory tests in strictly controlled conditions.

Schemas

Schemas are internal mental representations that allow us to organise thoughts, categorise events and predict outcomes. Our schemas start in early life and we add to them continually throughout life, developing new ones and altering those already there. New experiences either broadly fit with existing thinking (in which case we assimilate), or they may require alterations or entirely new schemas to be developed (in which case we accommodate).

Importantly, however, schemas are not always accurate representations of events or things. They are very much our own interpretation of these events and are as prone to distortion as our memories. Note: schemas for events are called scripts. Others include role schemas that tell us how to behave when performing different roles such as teacher, doctor, vicar etc.

Knowledge check 4

List three areas of research studied by cognitive psychologists.

Key study: Loftus and Palmer (1974)

The reliability of eyewitness memory

Elizabeth Loftus has conducted numerous studies investigating the accuracy of eyewitness testimony and has, on many occasions, testified in court about the factors that affect eyewitness memory.

Aim: To find out whether leading questions distort (change) an eyewitness memory of an event.

Method and design: Two laboratory experiments; both have independent design.

Independent variables:
- IV in experiment 1: the strength of the verb — contacted, bumped, collided, hit, smashed.
- IV in experiment 2: whether the leading question included the verb hit or smashed.

Participants:
- Experiment 1: 45 participants, all university students, randomly allocated to five groups of nine.
- Experiment 2: 150 participants, all university students, randomly allocated to three groups of 50.

Procedure:
- **Exp 1:** 45 participants watched a video of a car accident. Afterwards participants were asked to write an account of what they had seen, and then given a questionnaire which included the critical leading question. The participants were divided into five groups and each group received a different version of the critical question, either containing the verb 'smashed', 'collided', 'bumped', 'hit' or 'contacted'.
- **Exp 2:** 150 participants, in three groups of 50, were shown a film of a car accident and were given a questionnaire. Group 1 were asked the leading question containing the word 'hit', group 2 were asked it with the word 'smashed' and group 3 (the control group) were not asked a leading question. A week later the participants returned and were asked further questions, including the critical question 'Did you see any broken glass?' (there was no broken glass in the film).

Controls: All watched the same film in the same environment, all wrote a description of what they had seen before they were questioned. In experiment 2 there was a control group to establish a base line for the erroneous reporting of seeing broken glass.

→

Findings:

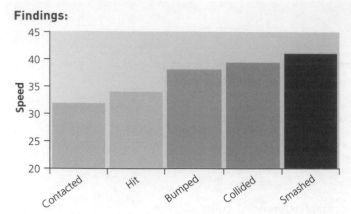

Figure 1 Experiment 1: estimated speed for verb used

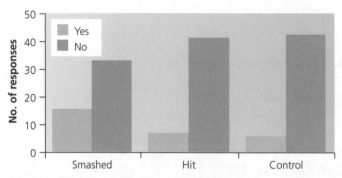

Figure 2 Experiment 2: response to 'Did you see any broken glass?'

Conclusion: The meaning of the verb used in the leading question (the semantics) had become integrated with the memory of the event, thus changing the memory and causing a false memory to be constructed. This shows that what happens after we have witnessed an event can alter our memory of the event.

Cognitive neuroscience

Cognitive neuroscience integrates the theories of cognitive science with approaches in experimental psychology, neuropsychology and neuroscience. It uses new technologies to 'measure the brain', including transcranial magnetic stimulation (TMS), EEG and advanced brain imaging methods such as MRI and PET scans. Integrative neuroscience creates unified descriptive models from fields such as biology, psychology, anatomy and clinical practice.

Advances in neuroimaging and associated data analysis methods have made it possible to research the relationship between thought processes and brain activity.

Key study: Maguire (2000)

Navigation related structural change in the hippocampi of London taxi drivers

Aim: To find out whether changes in the brain could be detected in those with extensive navigation experience.

Hypothesis: Based on research suggesting that the role of the hippocampus is to facilitate spatial memory (navigation): that the hippocampi in London taxi drivers will be structurally different to the hippocampi in non-taxi drivers.

Method: Natural experiment — independent design.

Participants: Two groups:
- Group 1: 16 right-handed, male taxi drivers, average age 44, all licensed more than 18 months, average time as taxi driver 14.3 years
- Group 2: 16 right-handed, male, age matched, non-taxi drivers

IV and DV:
- **IV:** London taxi driver (brain) or non-taxi driver (brain)
- **DV:** structure and volume of hippocampi

Procedure:
- **Stage 1:** MRI scans of brains of 50 healthy, right-handed, male, non-taxi drivers aged 33–61 were analysed to establish a comparison database of 'average hippocampi' (analysis by Voxel Based Morphometry (VBM)).
- **Stage 2:** MRI scans of brains of 16 taxi drivers and of 16 matched controls were analysed by VBM and compared to this database.
- **Control:** the expert conducting the analysis did not know whether each MRI scan was of a taxi driver brain or not. Fully informed consent was gained. All had healthy general medical, neurological and psychiatric profiles.

Findings: Increased volume of grey matter in both the right and left hippocampi in taxi driver brains, especially the right posteria hippocampus.

Correlational analysis found that the volume of the right posteria hippocampus increased as the length of time as a taxi driver increased. Taxi drivers had greater volume in the posteria hippocampus but non-taxi drivers had greater volume in the anterior hippocampus, indicating a redistribution of the grey matter in the hippocampus.

Conclusions:
- The structure of the brain changes in response to environmental demand.
- The mental map of the city of London is stored in the posteria hippocampi in taxi drivers.
- Normal activity can induce changes in the structure of the brain. This has many implications for rehabilitation after brain injury.

Exam tip

You should be able to explain why measuring mental processes is likely to be problematic.

> **Evaluation**
>
> **Strengths**
> - The cognitive approach focuses on how the individual experiences the world and on his or her feelings and beliefs rather than relying on interpretations by other people.
> - The approach is hopeful as it assumes people have the power to change their behaviour.
>
> **Limitations**
> - The approach may encourage the idea that people are responsible for their own psychological problems and this could lead to people being blamed for psychological abnormalities.
> - The approach is reductionist, as it ignores biological causes of psychological abnormality such as genetics and biochemistry.

Knowledge check 5

Outline the assumptions of the cognitive approach.

The biological approach

The biological approach assumes that there is a direct relationship between biology and behaviour and explores how behaviour is influenced by genetics, biochemistry and brain anatomy. The biological model is deterministic and takes the strictly 'nature' stance in the nature–nurture debate.

Biological psychologists use **scientific research methods**, often laboratory experiments because they allow for tight control of variables, testable hypotheses and cause and effect relationships to be established. Other research methods used by biological psychologists include:

- **Twin and family studies:** comparisons of MZ (identical) and DZ (non-identical) twins are used to determine whether or not behaviours are genetically or environmentally determined. If concordance rates for MZ are significantly higher than for DZ a genetic component is assumed. Comparisons between other family members can be used.
- **Brain scans:** these allow us to see which areas of the brain are active when we carry out certain activities. Methods include positron emission tomography (PET) scans, computer-aided tomography (CAT or CT) scans and magnetic resonance imaging (MRI) scans.
- **Chemical manipulation:** drugs may be administered to see how they influence behaviour. For example, the use of SSRI drugs in the treatment of depression.

The influence of genes

Our psychological characteristics are seen as a combination of nature and nurture, but the biological approach tends to emphasise the importance of genetic inheritance, for example geneticists assume that IQ is partially genetically determined. Heritability refers to the proportion of the characteristic that is seen as being genetic, and some disorders, such as schizophrenia, run in families. This suggests an underlying genetic cause. Kety et al. (1994) looked at a sample of adoptees with schizophrenia and found the incidence of the disorder was ten times higher in the biological relatives of the schizophrenic adoptees than in the biological relatives of the control group. Evidence of inheritance has also been found for eating disorders — Holland et al. (1984), in a study of twins, found a 55% concordance rate for identical twins compared to 7% for non-identical twins.

However, even if we inherit a gene the environment may influence the genetic effect:

- The **genotype** refers to the genetic makeup of an organism or group of organisms with reference to a single trait, or to the sum total of genes transmitted from parent to offspring.
- The **phenotype** refers to the observable physical characteristics of an organism as determined by both genetic makeup and environmental influence.

The expression of a trait, such as height, is based on genetic as well as environmental influence, thus a person can inherit a gene for 'tallness' (genotype) but because of malnourishment may not grow as tall as he or she would have done (phenotype).

Biological structures

Psychologists and neuroscientists associate certain brain areas with certain functions. There are two opposing theories of brain function:

- **Localisation of function:** the theory that functions such as memory, language, perception, attention etc. are located in specific brain areas. For example, the pre-frontal cortex is where attention 'happens', Broca's area is where speech production 'is done' and the hippocampus is somewhere that memory 'happens'.
- **Mass action:** in simple terms, the theory that functions such as memory are distributed throughout the brain and if one area is damaged, another area can take over. We now know that specific areas of the brain do have certain functions, but also that in any given behaviour, many parts of the brain all work together.

Neurochemistry (neurotransmitters)

Neurotransmitters are biochemicals that carry the signals between brain cells. Too much or too little of a neurotransmitter may result in psychological disorders. For example, too much dopamine is thought to lead to schizophrenia. Some examples of neurotransmitter substances are:

- **Adrenaline:** increases our levels of arousal and prepares us for a fast response, particularly in the case of an emergency.
- **Serotonin:** has a variety of roles, but is the 'feel-good' neurotransmitter that improves our mood and plays a role in getting us to sleep.
- **Dopamine:** involved in muscle movement, memory, emotion and schizophrenia.
- **Endorphins:** hormones (such as β-endorphin, pronounced beta-endorphin) which are involved in reducing perception of pain and stress, as well as pleasure (including sexual). Endorphins are chemically similar to morphine and are released at times of pain and during extreme exercise.

Knowledge check 6

Identify three biological influences on human behaviour.

Exam tip

You must be able to explain the difference between genotype and phenotype.

Knowledge check 7

Outline the assumptions of the biological approach.

Evaluation

Strengths

- The biological approach does not blame people for their psychological problems. This leads to a more humane treatment of the mentally ill.
- The scientific status and association with the medical profession means that this approach enjoys credibility.
- Objective evidence shows that biological causes can be linked to psychological symptoms, e.g. dopamine levels in schizophrenia.

Limitations

- Even if we know with certainty which part of the brain is active and how much activity there is, we can never be absolutely sure how the brain activity relates to behaviour. Does the brain activity cause the behaviour, or does the behaviour cause the brain activity?
- The approach gives a reductionist explanation for human behaviour, and ignores social and cognitive factors known to influence behaviour.

Exam tip

Make sure you can list three biological causes of behaviour.

Knowledge check 8

List three biochemical substances known to affect behaviour.

The psychodynamic approach

This topic is not examined at AS.

The psychodynamic approach assumes that behaviour is motivated by unconscious forces and by unresolved, unconscious conflicts. The model is based on Freud's proposal that the human personality comprises the id, the ego and the superego, and that the development of the personality progresses in five psychosexual stages (the oral, anal, phallic, latent and genital stages). According to the psychodynamic approach, in childhood the ego is not fully developed and cannot manage the conflicting demands of the id and the superego. Conflict and anxiety may result and the ego defends itself by repression, projection or displacement.

The unconscious mind

Freud's theory was that psychic energy motivates us and creates conflicts. Psychodynamic ('psycho' = mind and 'dynamic' = movement) refers to the constant movement of psychic energy within the mind and how this influences our thoughts and behaviours. Freud separated the mind into two parts: the conscious mind of which we are aware, and the unconscious mind that is unknown to us. He compared the conscious mind to the tip of an iceberg — the unconscious mind forms the larger part beneath the surface of conscious awareness and has a much greater impact on our personality.

The structure of the personality

- **Id.** This (instincts and drives) motivates people to seek pleasure while avoiding pain and to do so at whatever cost to others; it is selfish. The id operates on what Freud called the **pleasure principle** and is present at birth. The id in turn is driven by two other instinctive drives:
  - **eros** or life instinct, motivating us to behave in life preserving and life enhancing ways
  - **thanatos** or death instinct, which causes us to attack anyone that gets in the way

The id drives people to seek instant gratification and is happy for them to destroy anything that gets in their way.

- **Ego.** This develops to resolve the conflict arising from potty training during the anal stage of development. The ego represents what the conscious mind believes is the real 'us'. Operating on the **reality principle**, the ego is logical and seeks to maintain balance in a real world.

- **Superego.** This develops during the phallic stage as a resolution to the Oedipus complex or Elektra conflict. The superego operates on the **morality principle** and motivates people to behave in a socially responsible manner. Freud subdivided the superego into two parts, the **ego-ideal** which tells us how we should behave and the **conscience** which nags us when we do not. The superego influences personality and, like the id, it is mostly unconscious.

Freud believed that a strong ego was essential to psychological health and that our wellbeing depends on minimising conflict and satisfying the needs of the different parts of personality. If the id gains the upper hand we are likely to become selfish and antisocial, but if the superego becomes strongest we will be worried and moralistic.

Ego defence mechanisms

Ego defence mechanisms are operations of the unconscious mind. The real reasons underlying behaviour cannot be known. Examples of ego defence mechanisms are:

- **Repression.** Thoughts or desires that are upsetting or disturbing are locked away in the unconscious mind — though hidden from conscious thought they can still influence behaviour.

- **Displacement.** This usually involves anger, and anger is displaced or redirected towards a substitute. For example, anger at a sibling is displaced onto the dog. Freud suggested that displacement could be an explanation of depression — where anger is redirected against the self.

- **Projection.** Projecting your own unconscious unacceptable characteristics on to others. For example, according to Freud, Little Hans projected his unconscious wish that his mother drown his sister onto a fear that his mother would drown him in the bath.

- **Denial.** The person simply denies the existence of the problem, for example, those addicted to substances or gambling.

- **Sublimation.** The person channels unacceptable desires into positive behaviour, for example, aggression into sport. Freud believed all our positive attributes were sublimations of our sexual desires and drives.

- **Regression.** Faced with stress, people revert to an earlier, usually childhood, stage of development. For example, they may behave like a child and have a tantrum.

The psychosexual stages of development

Freud believed that as we develop our sexual or life energy (libido) we focus on different parts of the body. Each stage has an optimal level of satisfaction — too much or too little satisfaction in each stage leads to fixations that shape later personality.

- **Oral (0–2ish).** Children are born into this stage. Satisfaction centres on the mouth, eating and sucking. Too little oral satisfaction results in a person who is uncaring and in later life may develop behaviour such as smoking or nail-biting. Too much oral satisfaction results in a personality that is overly enthusiastic.

Exam tip

Make sure you can name and describe the three parts of the personality.

- **Anal (2–4ish).** Pleasure is now centred on the anus, particularly defecation. The ego develops in order to resolve conflict between the id (which wants instant pleasure and pooing at will) and parents who require restraint. Overly strict potty training results in an anally retentive personality where the person grows up to be obsessively tidy and organised.
- **Phallic (4–6ish).** Pleasure is now centred on the penis (boys). During the phallic stage the child starts to develop desires for the opposite sex parent. The boy's desire for the mother results in him wanting to take the place of the father (Oedipus complex). This causes anxiety since he believes if the father discovers his desire he will castrate him. A similar process — the Elektra conflict — occurs in girls. The Oedipal feelings are repressed until adolescence when they become displaced onto members of the opposite sex.
- **Latency (6ish to puberty).** An almost dormant period during which time the sexes go their separate ways and the child learns appropriate social and gender specific rules and patterns of behaviour.
- **Genital (puberty onwards).** Libido is now directed towards the genitals and sexual maturity begins.

Key study: Freud (1909)

Analysis of a phobia in a 5-year-old boy

Aim: To find out what caused Hans's phobia of horses and to collect evidence to support Freud's theories.

Method: Longitudinal case study. Hans's father wrote letters to Freud who analysed the information and wrote back. Freud only met Hans once.

Participant: A 5-year-old boy called Little Hans. His father was Max Graf, a supporter of Freud and member of the psychoanalytic society.

Procedure: Hans's father wrote to Freud when the boy was 5 years old, describing the main problem: 'He is afraid a horse will bite him in the street, and this fear seems somehow connected with his having been frightened by a large penis.'

- **Hans and his widdler:** Hans had an interest in that part of his body he called his 'widdler'.
- **Hans's mother and sister:** When Hans was 3½ his baby sister was born and he expressed hostility towards his new sister.
- **Hans's castration fear:** When his mother found him playing with his widdler she threatened that she would arrange for it to be cut off. Hans's father told him that women have no widdlers and Freud reasoned that this would lead Hans to think: 'Mother had a widdler before and now she hasn't. It must have been cut off. She said mine might be cut off if I touched it.' This would serve to confirm his fears of castration.
- **Hans's dreams and fantasies:** Hans told his father a dream about two giraffes — a big one and a crumpled one. Hans took away the crumpled one and this made the big one cry out. Hans sat down on the crumpled one. Hans's father thought that this was a representation of what happened in the mornings between Hans and his parents. Hans liked to get into his parents'

Knowledge check 9

Identify the psychosexual stages of personality development in the correct order.

Exam tip

You could be asked to describe examples of ego defence mechanisms.

bed but his father (the big giraffe) often objected. Hans took away his mother (the crumpled one), which caused his father to cry out. Hans sat on top of his mother to claim her for himself. Freud wondered if the giraffe's long neck represented the large adult penis.

- **The link between fear of horses and fear of father:** Freud suggested that Hans's fear of horses was actually a fear of his father. The black around the horses's mouths and the blinkers in front of their eyes were symbols for his father's moustaches and glasses.
- **Hans recalled a key memory:** He was walking with his mother when they saw a horse fall down and kick its legs about and Hans was afraid the horse was dead. What was the link with his father? Hans secretly wished his father would fall down dead — a desire that would have made him feel guilty and anxious at the same time.
- **Resolution:** Hans's fear of horses began to subside and Hans developed two final fantasies which showed that he had now resolved his feelings about his father. 'The plumber came and first he took away my behind with a pair of pincers, and then he gave me another, and then the same with my widdler.' This is taken to mean that Hans was given a bigger backside and widdler, like Daddy's.

Conclusion: Freud felt that the case study of Hans provided support for his ideas about infant sexuality. First, there was clear evidence of Hans's interest in sexual matters. Second, there was also evidence to support the idea of the Oedipus complex. Hans had a wish to be close to his mother and to engage in sexual relations with her. This set Hans up as a rival to his father and he wished him gone (dead). Successful resolution of the Oedipus conflict came when Hans was able to express his feelings about his father and was able to transfer his identification from his mother to his father.

Evaluation

Strengths

- The psychodynamic approach identifies the importance of traumatic childhood experience in adult problems.
- Freud's theories changed people's attitudes to mental illness. Psychosomatic illnesses demonstrate the link between mind and body.
- The approach does not hold people responsible for their behaviour, as the causes of behaviour are unconscious.

Limitations

- The approach is not scientific: Freud's theories are not falsifiable (his hypotheses are not testable).
- The approach overemphasises past experience, suggesting that past experience motivates current behaviour.
- The approach is reductionist and ignores biological and sociocultural factors.

Exam tip

In an exam you may need to explain why it is difficult to measure unconscious mental processes.

Knowledge check 10

Outline the assumptions of the psychodynamic approach.

Humanistic psychology

This topic is not examined at AS.

Free will, self-actualisation and Maslow's hierarchy of needs

Humanistic psychology was developed by Rogers and Maslow in the 1950s. It assumes that a healthy psychological attitude is dependent on taking personal responsibility, recognising the existence of **free will**, and striving towards personal growth and fulfilment. It also assumes that individuals have a need for **self-actualisation** and that people are naturally good, with the potential for personal growth if they are provided with appropriate circumstances. Another assumption is that if children receive **unconditional positive regard** they will develop satisfactorily, but if they experience **conditional regard**, they are prevented from realising their potential and becoming self-actualised. Humanistic psychologists rely on self-report methods, as they believe that psychologists should treat as 'evidence' how the individual reports his or her own conscious experiences.

Abraham Maslow believed that people have an inborn desire to be self-actualised, to be all they can be. He proposed a **hierarchy of needs** and suggested that people are motivated to fulfil basic needs before they can move on to more advanced needs. This hierarchy of needs can be seen as a pyramid.

Self-actualisation
Needs to fulfil potential

Aesthetic
Needs for order and beauty

Esteem
Needs for confidence, sense of worth and competence

Attachment
Needs to belong, affiliate, to love and be loved

Safety
Needs for security, comfort, tranquillity, freedom from fear

Biological
Needs for food, rest, sexual expression, release from tension

Figure 3 Maslow's hierarchy of needs

The lowest levels of the pyramid are made up of the most basic needs, while the more complex needs are located at the top of the pyramid. Needs at the bottom of the pyramid are basic physical requirements, including the need for food, water, sleep and warmth. Once these lower-level needs have been met, people can move on to the next level of needs, which are for safety and security.

As people progress up the pyramid, needs become increasingly psychological and social, such as the need for love, friendship, and intimacy. Further up the pyramid, the need for personal esteem and feelings of accomplishment take priority. Maslow emphasised the importance of self-actualisation, which is a process of growing and developing as a person in order to achieve individual potential.

Personality development: the self

Central to Rogers' personality theory is the notion of **self** or **self-concept**. This is defined as 'the organised, consistent set of perceptions and beliefs about oneself'. The self is influenced by the experiences a person has in his or her life, and our interpretations of those experiences. Two primary sources that influence our self-concept are childhood experiences and evaluation by others. According to Rogers (1959), we want to feel and behave in ways which are consistent with our self-image and which reflect what we would like to be like, our **ideal self**.

Self-concept includes three components:

- **Self-worth (self-esteem):** what we think about ourselves. Feelings of self-worth are developed in early childhood and are formed from the interaction of the child with the mother and father.
- **Self-image:** how we see ourselves, which is important to good psychological health. Self-image includes the influence of our body image on personality. Self-image has an effect on how a person thinks, feels and behaves in the world.
- **Ideal self:** this is the person who we would like to be. It consists of our goals and ambitions in life, and is forever developing. The ideal self in childhood is not the ideal self in adulthood.

Self-worth and positive regard

Rogers (1951) viewed a child as having two basic needs: positive regard from other people and self-worth. Our feelings of self-worth are of fundamental importance both to psychological health and to the likelihood that we can achieve self-actualisation. A person who has high self-worth, that is, has confidence and positive feelings about him- or herself, faces challenges in life, accepts failure and is open with people. A person with low self-worth may avoid challenges in life, not accept that life can be unhappy at times, and will be defensive and guarded with other people.

Rogers believed feelings of self-worth developed in early childhood and were formed from the interaction of a child with his or her parents:

- **Unconditional positive regard** is where parents accept and love their child for what he or she is. Positive regard is not withdrawn if the child does something wrong or makes a mistake. People who are able to self-actualise are more likely to have received unconditional positive regard from others, especially their parents in childhood.
- **Conditional positive regard** is where positive regard, praise and approval, depend on the child behaving in ways that the parents think correct. Hence the child is not loved for the person he or she is, but on condition that he or she behaves only in ways approved by the parents.

Congruence

A person's ideal self may not be consistent with what actually happens in life and experiences of the person. Hence, a difference may exist between a person's ideal self and actual experience. This is called **incongruence**. Where a person's ideal self and actual experience are consistent or very similar, a state of **congruence** exists. Rarely,

Knowledge check 11

Explain what is meant by self-actualisation.

Exam tip

You may need to be able to explain what is meant by self-concept/ self-esteem.

if ever, does a total state of congruence exist — all people experience a certain amount of incongruence.

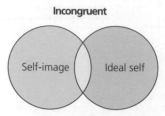
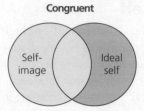

Incongruent

The self-image is different to the ideal self
There is only a little overlap
Here self-actualisation will be difficult

Congruent

The self-image is similar to the ideal self
There is more overlap
This person can self-actualise

Figure 4 Relationship between self-image and the ideal self

The development of congruence is dependent on **unconditional positive regard**. Rogers believed that for people to achieve self-actualisation they must be in a state of congruence. The closer our self-image and ideal self are to each other, the more consistent or congruent we are and the higher our sense of self-worth. People are said to be in a state of incongruence if some of the totality of their experience is unacceptable to them and is denied or distorted in their self-image. We prefer to see ourselves in ways that are consistent with our self-image, so a person whose self-concept is incongruent with his or her real feelings and experiences will use defence mechanisms because the truth hurts.

The influence on counselling

Therapy aims to uncover distortions and denials so the individual can gain insight into his or her true self. **Client-centred therapy** is based on the therapist giving the client unconditional positive regard, being genuine and honest and empathising. Humanistic theory has been incorporated into many differing views on psychotherapy and many argue now that humanistic counselling provides a foundation for individual change.

Evaluation

Advantages

- Humanistic psychology empowers individuals by emphasising free will and the ability to change.
- It formed the basis for client-centred therapy which is widely used and accepted as an effective treatment.
- Client-centred therapy provides insight into what an experience means to the individual.

Limitations

- It has been criticised as being culturally biased, appropriate only in Western culture where the emphasis is on individualism rather than collectivism.
- It ignores biological influences.
- It suggests that parenting is responsible for psychological problems.

Exam tip

You must be able to explain what is meant by 'a state of congruence' and 'a state of incongruence'.

Knowledge check 12

Outline the assumptions of the humanistic approach.

Exam tip

You may be given a hypothetical example of a person and asked to explain his or her behaviour from the humanistic approach.

Knowledge check 13

Define and explain the humanistic terminology: hierarchy of needs, unconditional positive regard, congruence and incongruence.

Comparison of approaches

This topic is not examined at AS.

Approach	Origin of behaviour	Criticism	Comment
Biological Behaviour is a symptom of an underlying biological cause.	Inside the person. It may be: ● inherited/genetic ● brain damage ● neurotransmission	Deterministic. Reductionist. No free will. Can't explain why talking cures or conditioning are effective.	Ignores psychosocial factors but is scientific. Does not 'blame' the individual. Treatment = drugs/ECT.
Behavioural Behaviour is learned and can be unlearned.	Behaviour is learned in interaction with the environment: ● classical or operant conditioning ● social learning theory	Deterministic/the past. No free will. Can't explain why drugs or talking cures work.	Ignores biological factors. Does not 'blame' the individual. Treatment based on conditioning (learning).
Psychodynamic Behaviour is a symptom of an unseen cause. Unconscious conflict between id, ego and superego.	Inside the person, during early years, e.g. Oedipus complex, ego defences such as repression, regression.	Deterministic/the past. No free will. Can't explain why drug treatment is effective. Not based on scientific evidence.	Ignores biological factors. Does not 'blame' the individual. Treatment = talking cure, psychoanalysis.
Cognitive Behaviour is the result of mental processes.	Inside the person: rational and irrational thoughts, attention, memory etc.	May 'blame' the individual: if you didn't think irrationally you wouldn't have a problem! Can't explain why drug treatment is effective.	Ignores biological and social factors. Treatment = talking cure, cognitive behavioural therapy (CBT).
Humanistic Behaviour is the result of the need to reach self-actualisation.	Inside the person: self-esteem, accepting (or not) the 'self' as it is.	Self-orientated — encourages selfishness. Culturally biased to individualistic cultures. Not based on scientific evidence.	Ignores biological factors. Treatment = talking cure, client-centred therapy.

Exam tip

The cognitive approach involves conscious thought processes; the psychodynamic approach involves unconscious thought processes. Do not confuse these.

Knowledge check 14

Explain what is meant by reductionism and determinism and accurately identify the approaches that can be described as reductionist and/or determinist.

Approaches to psychology: a glossary of terms

behavioural approach: an approach that sees the abnormal behaviour as the problem rather than as the symptom of an underlying cause. It makes three assumptions: first, that all behaviour is learned; second, that what has been learned can be unlearned; and third, that abnormal behaviour is learned in the same way as normal behaviour.

biological approach: an approach that assumes that psychological abnormalities are symptoms of underlying physical causes.

classical conditioning: stimulus–response learning following which a neutral stimulus causes reflex behaviour.

cognitive approach: an approach that proposes that to be normal is to be able to use cognitive processes to monitor and control our behaviour. By this view, abnormal behaviour is caused by faulty or irrational thoughts, or when people make incorrect inferences about themselves or others, and/or about themselves and the future.

humanistic approach: humanistic psychology assumes that a healthy psychological attitude is dependent on taking personal responsibility, recognising the existence of free will, and striving towards personal growth and fulfilment.

psychodynamic approach: the assumption that behaviour is motivated by unconscious forces, and that abnormal behaviour has its origins in unresolved, unconscious conflicts in early childhood. This approach (based on Freud's theories) suggests that the ego defends itself by repression, projection or displacement. In repression, anxiety is hidden from the conscious mind (repressed) in the unconscious, but stress in adulthood may trigger the repressed conflict, leading to psychological abnormality.

Knowledge summary

At AS and A-level you should be able to:
- describe the origins of psychology and understand what is meant by introspection
- describe and evaluate the assumptions of the behaviourist approach, and explain the learning approaches to behaviour
- describe and evaluate the assumptions of the cognitive approach, and explain what is meant by mental schema
- describe and evaluate the assumptions of the biological approach, and distinguish between genotype and phenotype

At A-level you should also be able to:
- describe and evaluate the assumptions of the psychodynamic approach, including the structure of personality, defence mechanisms and the psychosexual stages of development
- describe and evaluate the assumptions of humanistic psychologists, the role of free will, self-actualisation and Maslow's hierarchy of needs
- compare all these different approaches

Biopsychology

The divisions of the nervous system

The nervous system is broken down into two major systems: the central nervous system (CNS) and the peripheral nervous system.

The central nervous system

The central nervous system consists of the brain and the spinal cord. The brain is divided into two symmetrical hemispheres: left (language, the 'rational' half of the brain, associated with analytical thinking and logical abilities) and right (more involved with musical and artistic abilities). The brain is also divided into four lobes:

- frontal (motor cortex) — motor behaviour, expressive language, higher-level cognitive processes
- parietal (somatosensory cortex) — involved in the processing of touch, temperature and pain
- occipital (visual cortex) — interpretation of visual information
- temporal (auditory cortex) — understanding language, as well as memory and emotion

The brain and spinal cord act together. The area where the spinal cord joins the brain is the brainstem which is involved in life-sustaining functions. Damage to the brainstem is very often fatal. The brainstem includes the medulla oblongata, which controls heartbeat, breathing, blood pressure, digestion, the reticular activating system, involved in arousal and attention, sleep and wakefulness, and control of reflexes, and the cerebellum, which controls balance, smooth movement and posture.

The peripheral nervous system

The peripheral nervous system is divided into two sub-systems: the **somatic nervous system** whose primary function is to regulate the actions of the skeletal muscles and the **autonomic nervous system** which regulates primarily involuntary activity such as heart rate, breathing, blood pressure, and digestion. The **hypothalamus** controls the autonomic nervous system; it is located below the thalamus, just above the brainstem. The autonomic nervous system is further broken down into two complementary systems: the **sympathetic** and **parasympathetic nervous systems**.

The sympathetic nervous system

The sympathetic nervous system controls what has been called the **'fight or flight'** phenomenon because of its control over the necessary bodily changes needed when we are faced with a situation in which we may need to defend ourselves or escape.

In a fight or flight situation the sympathetic nervous system prepares the body: your heart rate quickens to get more blood to your muscles, your breathing becomes faster and deeper to increase your oxygen, your blood flow is diverted from your organs so digestion is reduced and your skin gets cold and clammy and your pupils dilate for

Knowledge check 15

Outline the functions of the central nervous system and the peripheral nervous system.

better vision. In an instant, your body is prepared either to defend or escape. If the situation was not dangerous after all, the body adjusts, but it is several minutes before the body returns to its normal state.

The structure and function of sensory, relay and motor neurons

A neuron is a specialised nerve cell that receives, processes and transmits information to other cells in the body. About 10,000 neurons die every day but since it is theorised that we start out with between 10 and 100 billion we only lose about 2% over our lifetime.

Relay and motor neurons

Neurons are only capable of carrying a message in one direction. Sensory neurons are **afferent neurons**, meaning they only **relay information to the brain**. Motor neurons are **efferent neurons**, meaning they **carry information from the brain** to the target. In certain instances, it would take too long for information to go to the brain and then come back with an action in response. Instead, **relay neurons** or **interneurons** relay information from sensory neurons to motor neurons, bypassing the brain.

Think about touching a hot kettle. If the signal went all the way to your brain and back, your hand would be much more damaged than the instant jerk away from the stove that usually happens.

When a receptor is stimulated, it sends a signal to the central nervous system, where the brain coordinates the response. But sometimes a very quick response is needed, one that does not need the involvement of the brain. This is a reflex action. Reflex actions are rapid and happen without us thinking. The process is as follows:

■ receptor detects a stimulus — such as a hot kettle
■ sensory neuron sends signal to relay neuron
■ motor neuron sends signal to effector
■ effector produces a response

Information comes to the neuron through the **dendrites** from other neurons. It then continues to the cell body (soma), which is the main part of the neuron. This contains the **nucleus** and maintains the life-sustaining functions of the neuron. The soma processes information and then passes it along the **axon**. At the end of the axon are bulb-like structures called terminal buttons (or synaptic knobs) that pass the information on to glands, muscles or other neurons.

Synaptic transmission

Information is carried by biochemical substances called **neurotransmitters**. The terminal buttons and the dendrites of other neurons do not touch, but instead pass the information containing neurotransmitters through a **synapse**. Once the neurotransmitter leaves the axon, and passes through the synapse, it is caught on the dendrite by receptor sites.

Knowledge check 16

What is the difference between a relay and a motor neuron?

Neurotransmitters play a role in the way we behave, learn, feel and sleep. Some play a significant role in mental health:

- Acetylcholine: involved in voluntary movement, learning, memory and sleep. Too much acetylcholine is associated with depression, and too little has been associated with dementia.
- Dopamine: correlated with movement, attention and learning. Too much dopamine has been associated with schizophrenia, and too little is associated with some forms of depression.
- Norepinephrine: associated with eating and alertness. Too little norepinephrine has been associated with depression, while an excess has been associated with schizophrenia.
- Epinephrine: involved in energy and glucose metabolism. Too little epinephrine has been associated with depression.
- Serotonin: plays a role in mood, sleep, appetite and impulsive and aggressive behaviour. Too little serotonin is associated with depression and some anxiety disorders, especially obsessive compulsive disorder.
- Gamma-amino butyric acid (GABA): inhibits excitation and anxiety. Too little GABA is associated with anxiety and anxiety disorders.
- Endorphins: involved in pain relief and feelings of pleasure and contentedness.

Neurotransmission: excitation and inhibition

Some neurons in the CNS release neurotransmitters that excite other neurons. Others inhibit (prevent) neuronal activity.

- **Excitatory neurotransmitters.** The neuron passing the message (the presynaptic neuron) generates the action potential (AP) to release a neurotransmitter which affects the neuron receiving the message (the postsynaptic neuron). What always causes a neuron to release any neurotransmitter (whether it is excitatory or inhibitory) is an action potential. All excitatory neurotransmitters cause sodium ions to flow in and the cell becomes less negative on the inside. These excitatory neurotransmitters create a local increase of permeability of sodium ion channels which leads to a local depolarisation that is known as an **excitatory postsynaptic potential (EPSP)** because we are exciting the postsynaptic cell.
- **Inhibitory neurotransmitters.** If an action potential goes down the synaptic knob of another neuron and releases an inhibitory neurotransmitter, it is going to be activating different receptor sites on the cell membrane of the postsynaptic cell. When an inhibitory neurotransmitter causes an opening of potassium ion channels this leads to an **inhibitory postsynaptic potential (IPSP)** because it is going to be less likely to generate an action potential.

Whether a neuron generates an action potential or not, depends on the **overall sum of EPSPs and IPSPs** occurring in the neuron at any moment in time.

The function of the endocrine system

The **endocrine system** consists of a set of glands that release chemical products into the bloodstream. **Glands** are organs or tissues in the body that produce chemicals that control many of our bodily functions. The endocrine glands consist of the

Knowledge check 17

List three neurotransmitter substances and their respective influences.

Exam tip

Make sure you can describe the process of synaptic transmission.

pituitary gland, the thyroid and parathyroid glands, the adrenal glands, the pancreas, the ovaries in women, and the testes in men. The chemical messengers produced by these glands are called **hormones**. The bloodstream carries hormones to all parts of the body, and the membrane of every cell has receptors for one or more hormones.

The **pituitary gland**, a pea-sized gland just beneath the hypothalamus, controls growth and regulates other glands. The front part of the pituitary is known as the master gland, because almost all of its hormones direct the activity of target glands elsewhere in the body. The pituitary gland is controlled by the hypothalamus.

The **adrenal glands**, located at the top of each kidney, regulate moods, energy level, and the ability to cope with stress. Each adrenal gland secretes **adrenaline** and **noradrenaline**. Unlike most hormones, adrenaline and noradrenaline act quickly. Adrenaline helps a person to get ready for an emergency by acting on smooth muscles, the heart, stomach, intestines and sweat glands. In addition, adrenaline arouses the sympathetic nervous system, and this system subsequently excites the adrenal glands to produce more adrenaline. Noradrenaline also alerts the individual to emergency situations by interacting with the pituitary and the liver. Noradrenaline functions as a neurotransmitter when it is released by neurons, but in the adrenal glands it is released as a hormone. The activation of the adrenal glands has an important role to play in the fight or flight response.

The **pancreas**, located under the stomach, is a dual-purpose gland that performs both digestive and endocrine functions. The part of the pancreas that serves endocrine functions produces a number of hormones, including insulin — the essential hormone that controls glucose (blood sugar) levels in the body and is related to metabolism and body weight.

The **ovaries**, located in the pelvis on either sides of the uterus in women, and **testes**, located in the scrotum in men, are the sex-related endocrine glands that produce hormones related to sexual development and reproduction.

The nervous system and endocrine system are intricately interconnected. The brain's hypothalamus connects the nervous system and the endocrine system and the two systems work together to control the body's activities. The endocrine system differs from the nervous system — the parts of the endocrine system are not all connected in the way that the parts of the nervous system are and the endocrine system works more slowly than the nervous system, because hormones are transported in our blood through the circulatory system.

> **Knowledge check 18**
>
> Name two glands in the endocrine system and outline their function.

The fight or flight response

To produce the fight-or-flight response, the hypothalamus activates two systems: the sympathetic nervous system and the adrenal-cortical system. The sympathetic nervous system uses nerve pathways to initiate reactions in the body, and the adrenal-cortical system uses the bloodstream. The combined effects of these two systems are the fight-or-flight response.

The fight or flight response originates in the **hypothalamus** and includes the pituitary and adrenal glands. This hypothalamic–pituitary–adrenal axis is responsible for arousing the autonomic nervous system (ANS) in response to a threat. The sympathetic branch of the nervous system stimulates the adrenal gland to release adrenaline, noradrenaline and corticosteroids into the bloodstream. The increase in adrenaline produces the physiological reactions, such as increased heart rate and blood pressure and a dry mouth, known as the 'fight or flight' response. After the threat is gone, it takes between 20 and 60 minutes for the body to return to its pre-arousal levels.

Localisation of function in the brain

This topic is not examined at AS.

The specialised functions of the brain

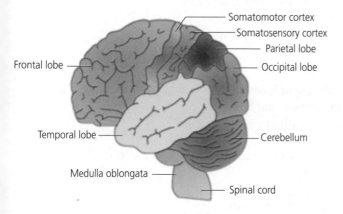

Figure 5 The brain

Located within the temporal lobe, the basal ganglia work with the cerebellum to coordinate fine motions, such as fingertip movements. The temporal lobe has a section called **Wernicke's area**, which is important for understanding the sensory (auditory and visual) information associated with language.

The **frontal lobe** is involved in motor skills (including speech) and cognitive functions. The motor centre of the brain, the **pre-central gyrus**, is located in the rear of the frontal lobe. It receives connections from the somatosensory portion in the parietal lobe and processes and initiates motor functions. Located within the temporal lobe, the **basal ganglia** work with the cerebellum to coordinate fine motions, such as fingertip movements.

Hemispheric lateralisation

The brain has two hemispheres which are connected by, and which communicate with each other via, the corpus callosum. **Lateralisation** is the theory that the left and right hemispheres are specialised to do different things. In general:

- The left hemisphere controls the right side of the body, is specialised for language and receives input from the *right* visual field.
- The right hemisphere controls the left side of the body, is specialised for spatial tasks and receives input from the *left* visual field.

Split-brain research: Roger Sperry (1968)

Aim: Sperry used split-brain patients to find out what happens when the two hemispheres cannot communicate with each other. The split-brain procedure involves cutting the corpus callosum which connects the two hemispheres. The operation is called a commisurotomy.

Participants: A group of individuals who suffered from severe epileptic seizures that could not be controlled by drugs. A commisurotomy was performed to help their epilepsy.

Procedure: Pictures were presented to the left or right visual field. The participant covered one eye and was instructed to look at a fixed point in the centre of a projection screen. Slides were projected onto either the right or left of the screen at a very high speed — one picture every 0.1 seconds or faster. Below the screen there was a gap so that the participant could reach objects but not see his or her hands.

Main findings:
- If a picture was first shown to the left visual field, the participant did not recognise it when the same picture appeared in the right visual field.
- If visual material appeared in the right visual field, the patient could describe it in speech and writing.
- If visual material appeared to the left visual field, the patient could identify the same object with their right hand but not their left hand.
- If visual material was presented to the left visual field, the patient consistently *reported* seeing nothing or just a flash of light to the left. However, the participant could point to a matching picture or object with his or her *right* hand. This confirms that the right hemisphere cannot speak or write (called *aphasia* and *agraphia*).

Additional findings:
- **$ and ?:** Sperry flashed two different pictures to the right and left visual fields: $ to the left and ? to the right. Participants would draw a dollar sign with their left hand. All participants would *say* that they saw the question mark and if they were asked what they had just drawn they would say the question mark (which was the wrong answer).
- **Key and case:** Sperry flashed composite words across the midline of the screen, such as 'key case', so that 'key' was in the left visual field, and 'case' in the right. If the participant was then given a group of objects to search through with his left hand, he would identify a key (because the left visual field goes to the right hemisphere which controls the left hand). With his right hand the participant would spell out the word 'case' (right visual field to left hemisphere which controls speech and the right hand). If the participant was now asked what kind of 'case' was being talked about, he had no idea that it might be a 'key case'. In other words, the left hemisphere did not know what was going on in the right hemisphere.
- **What is your left hand doing?** Another test involved asking participants to touch something with their left hand, and then identify it among a group of other objects with either their left or right hand. They could only do this with

Knowledge check 19

Outline two of the findings from the Roger Sperry split-brain study.

their left hand. If they were asked to say what they were holding they could not. In fact, they frequently said something like 'This hand is numb' or 'I don't get messages from that hand'.

If the experimenter told the participant that he had just successfully recognised the object with his left hand, he might say 'Well, I was just guessing'. If two objects were placed one in each hand and then the participant was given a pile of objects to search through, each hand would locate its own object.

- **Communication between hemispheres:** If participants saw an object in their left visual field (right hemisphere) they could not recognise it with their right hand. However, the right hemisphere (left hand) could still not recognise the objects because there is no language centre in the right hemisphere. If participants held an object in their left hand (right hemisphere) they could identify a picture of it as long as this was presented to their left visual field.
- **What the right (minor) hemisphere can do:** The right hemisphere is not totally word blind. Some split-brain patients, when shown words to their left visual field, could identify the item with their left hand (right hemisphere). However, they were still not able to say what it was. The right hemisphere was more responsive to emotion. If a nude figure was shown in among a series of geometric shapes, the participants typically denied seeing anything (left hemisphere is talking), but at the same time the participants might blush or display a cheeky grin (controlled by right hemisphere).

Conclusion: Sperry suggested that one hemisphere does not know what the other hemisphere is doing.

Exam tip

Make sure you can explain what the findings from the split-brain studies suggest about the functions of the left and right brain hemispheres.

Language centres in the brain

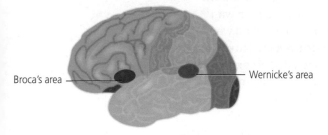

Broca's area ——— ——— Wernicke's area

Figure 6 Broca's area and Wernicke's area

An area on the left side of the frontal lobe, called **Broca's area**, processes language by controlling the muscles of the mouth, lips and larynx that control sound. If Broca's area is damaged the result is **motor aphasia**, in which patients can understand language, but cannot produce meaningful or appropriate sounds.

Wernicke's area is in the posterior part of the temporal lobe. Broca's area and Wernicke's area are connected by a bundle of nerve fibres called the arcuate fasciculus. Damage to the arcuate fasciculus causes a disorder called conduction aphasia. People with conduction aphasia can understand language, but their speech does not make sense and they cannot repeat words.

The occipital lobe receives and processes visual information from the eyes and relates this information to the parietal lobe (**Wernicke's area**) and motor cortex (frontal lobe). The temporal lobe processes **auditory information** from the ears and relates it to Wernicke's area of the parietal lobe and the motor cortex of the frontal lobe.

Brain plasticity

Brain plasticity refers to changes in neural pathways and synapses which occur as a result of changes in behaviour, environment and neural processes. The concept of neuroplasticity has replaced the formerly-held position that the brain is a physiologically static organ.

Neuroplasticity explores how the brain changes throughout life. It occurs on a variety of levels, ranging from cellular changes due to learning, to large-scale changes involved in cortical remapping in response to injury. The role of neuroplasticity is widely recognised in healthy development, learning, memory and recovery from brain damage. During most of the twentieth century, the general consensus among neuroscientists was that brain structure was relatively unchangeable after early childhood. However, research now indicates that experience can actually change both the brain's physical structure and functional organisation (refer to the study by Maguire on page 17). In a study in 2005, medical students' brains were imaged during the period when they were studying for their exams. In a matter of months, the students' grey matter increased significantly in the posterior and lateral parietal cortex.

Brain activity associated with a given function can also move to a different location in the brain in the process of recovery from brain injury. This is a theory that may explain improvements in stroke patients after physical therapy. Research suggests that brain plasticity can also be taken advantage of to counteract the effects of ageing.

Research evidence: Merzenich (1996)

Merzenich developed a series of plasticity-based computer programs known as FastForWord®. FastForWord® offers seven brain exercises to help with language and learning deficits. In a recent study, experimental training was done in adults to see if it would help to counteract the negative plasticity that results from age-related cognitive decline. The training included six exercises designed to reverse the dysfunctions caused by decline in cognition, memory and motor control. After use of the program for 8–10 weeks, there was a significant increase in task-specific performance. The data collected from the study indicated that a neuroplasticity-based program could improve cognitive function.

Ways of studying the brain

This topic is not examined at AS.

Functional magnetic resonance imaging (fMRI)

Magnetic resonance imaging (MRI) is a non-invasive medical test that helps physicians to diagnose and treat medical conditions. MRI uses a powerful magnetic field, radio frequency pulses and a computer to produce detailed pictures of organs, soft tissues and internal body structures. The images can then be examined on a computer monitor, transmitted electronically, printed and so on.

Functional magnetic resonance imaging (fMRI) is a relatively new procedure that uses MR imaging to measure the tiny metabolic changes that take place in an active part of the brain. This technique is becoming the diagnostic method of choice for learning how a normal, diseased or injured brain is working, as well as for assessing the potential risks of surgery or other invasive treatments of the brain. Physicians perform fMRI to examine the anatomy of the brain and to determine which part of the brain is handling critical functions such as thought, speech, movement and sensation (brain mapping). It is also used to assess the effects of stroke, trauma or degenerative disease on brain function and to monitor the growth and function of brain tumours.

Electroencephalogram (EEG)

Electroencephalography (EEG) is the recording of the electrical activity along the scalp. It measures voltage fluctuations resulting from ionic current flows within the neurons of the brain. EEG is often used to diagnose epilepsy which causes obvious abnormalities in EEG readings, and to diagnose sleep disorders and brain death. EEG used to be a first-line method of diagnosis for tumours and other focal brain disorders but this use has decreased with the advent of techniques such as fMRI and CT scans. EEG techniques include measuring evoked potentials (EPs), which involves averaging the EEG activity in response to the presentation of a stimulus of some sort (e.g. visual, somatosensory or auditory).

Event-related potentials (ERPs) refer to averaged EEG responses to more complex processing of stimuli. An ERP is the measured brain response that is the direct result of a specific sensory, cognitive or motor event — or put simply an ERP is any stereotyped electrophysiological response to a stimulus. The study of the brain using EEG provides a non-invasive means of evaluating brain functioning in patients with cognitive diseases.

Post-mortem studies

Post-mortem researchers often conduct a study of the brain of an individual who has some sort of affliction (e.g. cannot speak, trouble moving left side of body, Alzheimer's). Researchers look at certain lesions in the brain that could have an influence on cognitive functions. The irregularities or damage observed in the brain are studied in relation to the individual's illness, lifestyle and environment.

Post-mortem studies provide a unique opportunity for researchers to study the brain in ways that cannot be studied on a living person. They allow researchers to determine causes and cures for certain diseases and functions and to develop hypotheses to associate the location in the brain with specific behaviour. A benefit of post-mortem studies is that researchers have the ability to make a wide range of discoveries, because of the many different techniques used to obtain tissue samples. A disadvantage of post-mortem studies is that if changes are found in the brain we cannot know whether these changes caused, or resulted from, behaviour. Also, post-mortem brain samples are limited because it is extremely difficult for a researcher to get hold of an individual's brain as participants or families may not give their consent.

Knowledge check 21

Outline three ways of studying the brain.

Exam tip

You could be given a hypothetical scenario and asked to (a) suggest how you would measure the brain activity and (b) explain why you would choose the method you described.

Biological rhythms

This topic is not examined at AS.

Circadian rhythms

The word 'circadian' stems from the Latin *circa* (meaning 'about') and *diem* (meaning 'day'). There are some cycles that we are consciously aware of — the sleep/wake cycle being an obvious one — but other cycles we are not aware of. For example, our body temperature fluctuates over a 24-hour period. Generally it peaks mid-afternoon at about 37.1 C° and troughs in the small hours at about 36.7 C°.

Biological basis of circadian rhythms

In non-human species, the pineal gland appears to be the brain structure responsible for regulating the circadian sleep/wake cycle. In humans, the suprachiasmatic nucleus (SCN) appears to control the sleep/wake cycle. The SCN is situated in the hypothalamus just behind the eyes and receives sensory input about light levels through the optic nerve. The SCN appears to be the location of the main 'body clock'.

Internal (endogenous) pacemakers

To study endogenous pacemakers it is necessary to isolate people from external cues for many months. Over the past 40 years, the French geologist Michael Siffre has regularly spent extended periods of time in various caves around the world and has been studied during this process. In 1962 he spent 61 days in a cave in the Alps — he emerged in September but thought it was August and had lost 28 days. In 1972 and in 1999 he was again monitored in caves. Each time his body clock extended from the usual 24 hours which appears to suggest:

- There is internal control (endogenous) of the circadian rhythm because even in the absence of external cues we are able to maintain a regular daily cycle.
- There must usually be some external cue that keeps this cycle to 24 hours because when this is removed we adopt a 24.5 or 25-hour cycle.

External pacemakers (exogenous zeitgebers)

Light appears to be crucial in maintaining the 24-hour circadian rhythm. Campbell and Murphy (1998) shone bright lights onto the back of participants' knees and were able to alter their circadian rhythms in line with the light exposure. The exact mechanism for this is unclear, but it seems possible that the blood chemistry was altered and this was detected by the SCN.

Miles et al. (1977) reported the case study of a blind man who had a daily rhythm of 24.9 hours. Zeitgebers such as clocks and radios failed to reset the endogenous clock and the man relied on stimulants and sedatives to maintain a 24-hour sleep/wake cycle. Luce and Segal (1966) found that on the Arctic Circle people maintain a reasonably constant sleep pattern, averaging 7 hours a night, despite 6 months of darkness in the winter months, followed by 6 months of light in the summer. In these conditions it appears to be social factors that act to reset endogenous rhythms rather than light levels.

Infradian rhythms

Infradian rhythms occur over a period of time greater than 24 hours. There are a number of rhythms that are cyclic over about 1 year. In the animal world, examples include

> **Knowledge check 22**
>
> State the difference between circadian, infradian and ultradian rhythms.

migration, mating patterns and hibernation. In humans, the best example of an infradian rhythm is the **menstrual cycle** which lasts about 1 month and appears to be under the influence of both internal (**endogenous**) mechanisms and external zeitgebers. The cycle is under the internal (endogenous) control of hormones, particularly oestrogen and progesterone, secreted by the ovaries, but can also be influenced by external factors (zeitgebers), most notably by living with other women. The most likely mechanism for this is the action of pheromones — chemical substances similar to hormones.

Ultradian rhythms

An ultradian rhythm is one that repeats itself over a period of less than 24 hours. Ultradian rhythms occur more than once in a 24-hour cycle and most are confined to either day or night, for example the stages of sleep.

The stages of sleep

Sleep is an example of an ultradian rhythm as the cycle of sleep typically lasts about 90 minutes and during a typical night's sleep we will repeat this cycle four or five times. The stages of sleep can be monitored using EEG.

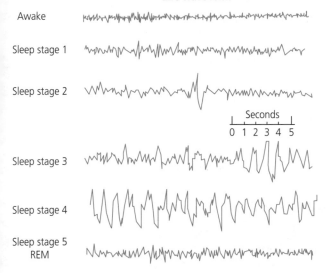

Figure 7 The stages of sleep

- **Awake.** The brain is active and shows what is called desynchronised beta activity.
- **Stage 1 sleep (15 minutes).** This occurs at the start of a night's sleep and lasts a matter of minutes. Brain waves are slower and are called 'theta'.
- **Stage 2 sleep (20 minutes).** This is characterised by bursts of high frequency waves called sleep spindles and at this stage we are still very easily woken.
- **Stage 3 sleep (15 minutes).** The brain waves start to slow and become higher in amplitude and wavelength. These 'delta waves' are associated with deep sleep and we are now more difficult to wake.
- **Stage 4 sleep (30 minutes).** Delta waves now constitute most of the brain activity and we are now at our most relaxed and are very difficult to wake up. Heart rate and blood pressure fall, muscles are very relaxed and temperature is at its lowest.

Exam tip

You might be asked to give an example of a circadian rhythm.

Exam tip

Make sure you can outline the stages of sleep and explain why this is an example of an ultradian rhythm.

■ **Stage 5 REM sleep (rapid eye movement).** REM is strange because the brain now becomes very active, almost indistinguishable from a waking brain. Heart rate and blood pressure increase and the eyes move rapidly giving this stage its name. Stages 1–4 are Non-REM (NREM) sleep.

Our first REM sleep lasts for about 10 minutes and then we start our journey back down to stage 2, stage 3 and stage 4 sleep. This cycle repeats throughout the night. There are large individual differences between people and some may sleep for much shorter periods, but others who have been sleep deprived will spend longer in stage 4 and REM sleep.

Biopsychology: glossary of terms

adrenal glands: these regulate moods, energy levels and the ability to cope with stress.

adrenaline and **noradrenaline:** fast-acting hormones. Adrenaline prepares the body for an emergency by acting on smooth muscles, the heart, stomach, intestines and sweat glands. Noradrenaline alerts the individual to emergency situations by interacting with the pituitary and the liver.

biopsychology: an area of psychology that focuses on understanding the relationship between biology and behaviour.

brain plasticity: the changes in neural pathways and synapses caused by changes in behaviour, environment and neural processes.

Broca's area: in the left hemisphere, this part of the brain processes language by controlling the muscles of the mouth, lips and larynx that control sound.

circadian rhythms: cycles of behaviour occurring every 24 hours (daily).

commissurotomy: the surgical operation to cut the corpus callosum to disconnect the left and right hemispheres.

dendrites: neurons have dendrites and information is passed through the dendrites to other neurons.

endocrine system: a set of glands that release chemicals such as hormones into the bloodstream.

endogenous pacemakers: internal (biological) pacemakers that regulate circadian or other rhythms.

excitatory neurotransmitters: these excite (activate) other neurons.

exogenous zeitgebers: external pacemakers such as light and dark that regulate circadian rhythms such as the sleep/wake cycle.

fight or flight response: the rapidly occurring physiological reactions that mobilise the body's resources to deal with threatening circumstances, such as increased heart rate and blood pressure and a dry mouth.

functional magnetic resonance imaging (fMRI): used to examine the anatomy of the brain and to determine which part of the brain is active and the level of brain activity.

Knowledge check 23

What is the difference between REM sleep and NREM sleep?

hemispheres: the brain has two hemispheres — the left hemisphere and the right hemisphere. The left hemisphere controls the right side of the body. The right hemisphere controls the left side of the body.

infradian rhythms: cycles of behaviour occurring over a period of time greater than 24 hours (e.g. the menstrual cycle in women).

inhibitory neurotransmitters: these prevent neuronal activity.

lateralisation: the theory that the left and right hemispheres of the brain are specialised to do different things.

localisation of function: the theory that each part of the brain is specialised to perform a specific function.

menstrual cycle: an example of an infradian rhythm.

motor neurons: efferent neurons which send messages from the brain to the body.

neurotransmitter substances: biochemical substances that influence how we behave, such as serotonin or dopamine.

NREM sleep: stages 1, 2, 3 and 4 of the sleep cycle comprising slow wave, synchronised brain activity.

pancreas: this gland performs both digestive and endocrine functions.

peripheral nervous system: the peripheral nervous system is divided into two sub-systems — the somatic nervous system whose function is to regulate the actions of the skeletal muscles and the autonomic nervous system which regulates primarily involuntary activity such as heart rate, breathing, blood pressure and digestion.

pituitary gland: a gland just beneath the hypothalamus that controls growth and regulates other glands.

post-mortem studies: a way of studying the brain after a person has died.

relay neurons (interneurons): these relay information from sensory neurons to motor neurons, bypassing the brain.

REM sleep: the stage of sleep in which desynchronised brain activity and rapid eye movements occur.

sensory neurons: afferent neurons which send messages from the body to the brain.

synapse: the gap between the terminal button of one neuron and a receptor of the next.

ultradian rhythms: a cycle of behaviour that repeats itself over a period of less than 24 hours.

Wernicke's area: in the left hemisphere, this part of the brain is important for understanding the meaning of language.

Knowledge summary

At AS and A-level you should be able to identify, describe, give examples of and explain:
- the divisions of the nervous system
- the structure and function of sensory, relay and motor neurons, the process of synaptic transmission and the role of neurotransmitters
- the function of the endocrine system — glands and hormones and the role of adrenaline in the fight or flight response

At A-level you should also be able to identify, describe, give examples of and explain:
- the localisation of function in the brain and hemispheric lateralisation
- the visual, auditory and language centres (Broca's and Wernicke's areas) and split-brain research

- plasticity and functional recovery of the brain after trauma
- ways of studying the brain: scanning techniques, including functional magnetic resonance imaging (fMRI), electroencephalogram (EEGs), event-related potentials (ERPs) and post-mortem examinations
- biological rhythms: circadian, infradian and ultradian and the difference between these rhythms
- the effect of endogenous pacemakers and exogenous zeitgebers on the sleep/wake cycle

■Research methods

Psychologists use many methods to conduct research. Each method has advantages and limitations, and the method selected needs to be appropriate for the topic of research. **Quantitative research** uses methods that measure amounts of behaviour, usually by assigning a numeric value to what is being measured (the quantity). **Qualitative research** measures what behaviour is like (the quality) and usually results in descriptive data. Quantitative data are collected as numbers, and qualitative data are collected as descriptions. You are expected to demonstrate knowledge and understanding of research methods, scientific processes and techniques of data handling and analysis, and be familiar with their use and be able to evaluate their strengths and limitations.

Experimental method

Laboratory experiments

A **laboratory experiment** is a method of conducting research in which researchers try to control all the variables except the one that is changed between the experimental conditions. The variable that is changed is called the **independent variable** (IV) and the effect it may have is called the **dependent variable** (DV). So the IV is manipulated and its effect (the DV) is measured. Laboratory experiments are conducted in controlled and often artificial settings.

> **Exam tip**
>
> Students often confuse the IV with the DV — make sure you can define both.

Evaluation

Strengths
- High levels of control in a laboratory experiment allow extraneous variables that might affect the IV or the DV to be minimised. The researcher can be sure that any changes in the DV are the result of changes in the IV.
- High levels of control make it possible to measure the effect of one variable on another. Statements about cause and effect can be made.
- Laboratory experiments can be replicated to check the findings with either the same or a different group of participants.

Weaknesses
- Laboratory experiments may not measure how people behave outside the laboratory in their everyday lives. Some experimental settings and tasks are contrived; hence the findings may have low internal validity.
- Aspects of the experiment may act as cues to behaviour that cause the participants (and the experimenter) to change the way they behave (demand characteristics), sometimes because of what they think is being investigated or how they think they are expected to behave. This can mean that it is not the effect of the IV that is measured, leading to invalid results.

Field experiments

A **field experiment** is a way of conducting research in an everyday environment (e.g. in a school or hospital), where one or more IVs are manipulated by the experimenter and the effect on the DV is measured. One difference between laboratory and field experiments is an increase in the naturalness of the setting and a decrease in the level of control that the experimenter is able to achieve. The key difference is the extent to which participants know they are being studied. Participants are aware of being studied in some field experiments, but this is not true of most, which is why participants' behaviour is more natural.

Exam tip

You should be able to explain why it may be an advantage to carry out research in the real world rather than in a laboratory.

Evaluation

Strengths

- Field experiments allow psychologists to measure how people behave in their everyday lives. The findings may have high external validity.
- Manipulation of the IV and some level of control make it possible to measure the effect of one variable on another. Statements about cause and effect can be made.
- If participants do not know they are participating in a study, they will be unaware that they are being watched or manipulated. This reduces the probability that their behaviour results from demand characteristics. However, this may not be true of all field experiments; the extent to which demand characteristics are present will vary depending on the experimental setting.

Weaknesses

- It is not always possible to control for extraneous variables that might affect the IV or the DV. The researcher cannot always be sure that any changes in the DV are the result of changes in the IV.
- Field experiments can be difficult to replicate and thus it may not be possible to check the reliability of the findings.
- It may not be possible to ask participants for their informed consent, and participants may be deceived and may not be debriefed, all of which are breaches of British Psychological Society ethical guidelines.

Knowledge check 24

In an experiment into the primacy recency effect, 25 student participants were seated in a quiet room and given a list of 20 four-letter words. All had 1 minute to memorise the words and then 1 minute to write down as many as they could remember. Suggest whether this is a laboratory experiment or a field experiment.

Natural (quasi) experiments

A **natural experiment** is one in which, rather than being manipulated by the researcher, the IV to be studied is naturally occurring. Some examples of naturally occurring variables are gender, age, ethnicity, occupation and smoker or non-smoker. When the IV is naturally occurring, participants cannot be randomly allocated between conditions. Just to complicate matters, a natural experiment may take place in a laboratory or in a field experimental setting.

Strengths

- Natural experiments allow psychologists to study the effects of IVs that could be unethical to manipulate.
- When participants are unaware of the experiment, and the task is not contrived, research may have high internal validity.

Weaknesses

- Since participants cannot be allocated randomly between conditions, it is possible that random variables (individual differences other than the IV) can also affect the DV. This may lead to low internal validity.
- Natural experiments can be difficult to replicate with a different group of participants. It may not be possible to check the reliability of the findings.

Exam tip

Make sure you know the difference between a laboratory experiment, a field experiment and a natural experiment and can list the strengths and weaknesses of each research method.

Knowledge check 25

A psychologist wanted to investigate the effect of two different types of childcare on children's social development. Ten children had attended a day nursery for a year and ten children had been looked after by a child minder for a year. All the children were 3 years old. Each child's mother completed a questionnaire. Explain why this is a natural experiment.

Observational techniques

When psychologists conduct an **observation**, they usually watch people's behaviour but remain inconspicuous and do nothing to change or interfere with it.

Types of observation

The following types of observation can be carried out.

- **Naturalistic observation.** People or animals are observed in their natural environment, without any sort of intervention or manipulation of variables and without their knowledge.
- **Controlled observation.** The researcher manipulates the behaviour of the observers or the observed, for example the Milgram study can be described as a controlled observation. This allows for greater control of confounding variables meaning it is easier to establish cause and effect relationships.
- **Overt observation.** Participants know they are being observed. This reduces ethical issues of consent and privacy, but reduces validity due to increased demand characteristics.
- **Covert observation.** Participants are unaware of the observation. This raises ethical issues (privacy and consent), but increases validity by reducing demand characteristics. Sometimes one-way mirrors might be used to discretely observe people, for example shopping behaviour in a supermarket.
- **Participant observation.** Here the researchers get involved with the group of participants they are observing.
- **Non-participant observation.** Participants are observed from a distance rather than the researchers infiltrating the group.

Evaluation

Strengths

- Behaviour can be observed in its usual setting and there are usually no problems with demand characteristics unless the situation in which the participants are being observed has been specially contrived.
- It is useful when researching children or animals.
- It can be a useful way to gather data for a pilot study.

Weaknesses

- No explanation for the observed behaviour is gained because the observer counts instances of behaviour but does not ask participants to explain why they acted as they did.
- Observers may 'see what they expect to see' (**observer bias**) or may miss, or misinterpret, behaviour.
- Studies are difficult to replicate.

Knowledge check 26

Outline two ways that psychologists use observational research methods.

Self-report techniques

One way to find out about people's behaviour is to ask them, and psychologists often do this. However, one of the main problems with asking questions about behaviour is that we all like others to think well of us. As a result, what we say about our behaviour and how we actually behave may be different. This is called **social desirability bias**.

There are several different ways in which psychologists design and conduct interviews and surveys.

Interviews

Structured interviews

All participants are asked the same questions in the same order. Structured interviews can be replicated and can be used to compare people's responses. However, they can be time consuming and require skilled researchers. People's responses can be affected by social desirability bias.

Unstructured interviews

In unstructured interviews, participants can discuss anything freely and the interviewer devises new questions on the basis of answers given previously. They provide rich and detailed information, but they are not replicable and people's responses cannot be compared. They can also be time consuming and people's responses can be affected by social desirability bias.

Questionnaires

Questionnaires are usually written, but they can be conducted face to face, or completed over the telephone, or on the internet. Printed questionnaires are completed by participants and are similar to structured interviews in that all participants are asked the same questions in the same order. They usually restrict participants to a narrow range of answers.

Questionnaires are a practical way to collect a large amount of information quickly and they can be replicated. Problems can arise if the questions are unclear or if they suggest a 'desirable' response, as responses can be affected by social desirability bias. When closed questions are used, participants cannot explain their answers.

Exam tip

Both questionnaires and interviews involve participant self-reporting. In the exam you could be asked to explain an advantage and disadvantage of (a) using questionnaires rather than interviews or (b) interviews rather than questionnaires.

Evaluation

Strengths

- Questionnaires can be used with large samples of participants.
- Structured interviews and questionnaires allow research to be replicated to test its reliability.
- Interviews allow rich detailed information to be gathered 'first hand' directly from the participants.

Weaknesses

- Self-report techniques cannot assume that participants will tell the truth — bias such as social desirability bias may lead to invalid results.
- Questionnaires or interviews may include leading questions that cause response bias.

Knowledge check 27

A psychologist wanted to investigate the effects of two different types of childcare on child development. Mothers of children who either attended a day nursery or who were looked after by a child minder were given a questionnaire. Write a suitable closed question that would produce quantitative data.

Correlations

Correlation is a statistical technique used to calculate the correlation coefficient in order to quantify the strength of relationship between two variables. An example is whether there is a relationship between aggressive behaviour and playing violent video games. However, studies that use correlational analysis cannot draw conclusions about cause and effect. If a relationship is found between behaving aggressively and playing violent video games, individual differences in personality variables could be one factor that causes both of these. Just because two events (or behaviours) occur together does not mean that one necessarily *causes* the other.

Analysis of the relationship between co-variables

The **correlation coefficient** is a mathematical measure of the degree of relatedness between sets of data. Once calculated, a correlation coefficient will have a value between −1 and +1. A **perfect positive correlation**, indicated by +1, is where as variable *X* increases, variable *Y* increases. A perfect negative correlation, indicated by −1, is where as variable *X* decreases, variable *Y* decreases.

Correlational data can be plotted as points on a scattergram. A line of best fit is then drawn through the points to show the trend of the data:

- If both variables increase together, this is a **positive correlation**.
- If one variable increases as the other decreases, this is a **negative correlation**.
- If no line of best fit can be drawn, there is **no correlation**.

Exam tip

In the exam you could be given a scattergram and asked to explain the findings shown. Make sure you can draw and label a scattergram and can interpret data shown on a scattergram.

Exam tip

Sketch three scattergrams, one showing a positive correlation, one showing a negative correlation and one showing no correlation.

Evaluation

Strengths

- Correlational analysis allows researchers to calculate the strength of a relationship between variables as a quantitative measure. A coefficient of +0.9 indicates a strong positive correlation; a coefficient of −0.3 may indicate a weak negative correlation.
- Where a correlation is found, it is possible to make predictions about one variable from the other.

Weaknesses

- Researchers cannot assume that one variable causes the other.
- Correlation between variables may be misleading and can be misinterpreted.
- A lack of correlation may not mean there is no relationship, because the relationship could be non-linear. For example, there is a relationship between physiological arousal and performance, but the relationship is expressed by a curve, not by a straight line. The Yerkes–Dodson curve shows that a little arousal improves performance, but too much reduces performance.

Knowledge check 28

If a correlation cooefficient between hours spent revising and scores on a psychology test is found to be +0.85 what would this suggest?

Case studies

This is not examined on AS papers.

A case study is a very detailed study into the life and background of one person (or of a small group of people). Case studies involve looking at past records, such as school and health records, and asking other people about the participant's past and present behaviour. They are often done on people who have unusual abilities or difficulties, e.g. Thigpen and Cleckley's three faces of Eve.

Evaluation

Strengths

- Case studies give a detailed picture of an individual and help to discover how a person's past may be related to his/her present behaviour.
- They can form a basis for future research.
- By studying the unusual we can learn more about the usual.

Weaknesses

- They can only tell you about one person so findings can never be generalised.
- The interviewer may be biased and/or the interviewee may not tell the truth.
- Retrospective studies may rely on memory, which may be inaccurate or distorted, and past records may be incomplete.

Exam tip

Make sure you can explain one strength and one weakness each of using the interview, questionnaire and case study methods.

Content analysis

This is not examined on AS papers.

Content analysis studies human behaviour indirectly by studying the things we produce, such as newspaper articles, television programmes and magazines. An analysis of the sources we produce tells us a lot about the way that our society is structured and about the beliefs, prejudices and values of our society.

Research evidence: Manstead and McCulloch (1981)

Manstead and McCulloch watched 170 television advertisements in a week and scored them on a whole range of factors such as:
- gender of product user
- gender of person in authority
- gender of person providing the technical information
- the type of product being advertised

They found that women were more likely to be portrayed as product users and to be cast in dependent roles and to be situated at home. Men were more likely to be portrayed as product experts and as authority figures.

Evaluation

Strengths
- Content analysis can produce large quantities of detailed and easily analysed material about a particular aspect of society.
- Replication is possible if details of the sources (the content) and how the analysis was conducted are published.

Weaknesses
- Observers carrying out the analysis may be biased. To avoid bias more than one observer should be used with inter-rater reliability being established.
- The choice of content to be analysed also introduces a source of bias.

Knowledge check 29

What type of data (qualitative or quantitative) are usually analysed in case studies and/or in content analysis?

Knowledge summary

At AS and A-level you should be able to:
- describe and evaluate experimental research methods, including laboratory, field and natural experiments
- describe and evaluate non-experimental research methods, including correlational analysis, observational techniques, self-report techniques including questionnaire and interview

At A-level you should also be able to:
- describe and evaluate case studies, and content analysis

■ Scientific processes

You should demonstrate knowledge and understanding of the way that psychologists carry out research and be able to describe and explain the scientific processes involved in research.

Ethics

Ethical research

Psychological research seeks to improve our understanding of human nature, and ethics are standards regarding what is right or wrong. An ethical issue occurs when there is conflict, for example, between what the researcher wants in order to conduct valid or meaningful research and the rights of participants.

Ethical guidelines

The British Psychological Society (BPS) has issued a set of ethical guidelines for research involving human participants. These ethical guidelines are designed to protect the wellbeing and dignity of research participants. The following guidelines are adapted from 'Ethical principles for conducting research with human participants'. The complete text is available on the website of the British Psychological Society (www.bps.org.uk).

BPS ethical guidelines

Introduction

Good psychological research is possible only if there is mutual respect and confidence between investigators and participants. Ethical guidelines are necessary to clarify the conditions under which psychological research is acceptable.

General

In all circumstances, investigators must consider the ethical implications and psychological consequences for the participants in their research. It is essential that the investigation should be considered from the standpoint of all participants; and foreseeable threats to their psychological wellbeing, health, values or dignity should be eliminated.

Consent

Whenever possible, the investigator should inform all participants of the objectives of the investigation. The investigator should inform the participants of all aspects of the research or intervention that might reasonably be expected to influence willingness to participate. Where

research involves any persons under 16 years of age, consent should be obtained from parents or from those in loco parentis.

Deception

The misleading of participants is unacceptable if the participants are typically likely to object or show unease once debriefed. Where this is in any doubt, appropriate consultation must precede the investigation. Consultation is best carried out with individuals who share the social and cultural background of the participants. Intentional deception of the participants over the purpose and general nature of the investigation should be avoided whenever possible.

Debriefing

Where the participants are aware that they have taken part in an investigation, when the data have been collected the investigator should provide the participants with any necessary information to complete their understanding of the nature of the research.

Withdrawal from the investigation

At the onset of the investigation, investigators should make plain to participants their right to withdraw from the research at any time, irrespective of whether or not payment or other inducement has been offered. The participant has the right to withdraw retrospectively any consent given, and to require that their own data, including recordings, be destroyed.

Confidentiality

Subject to the requirements of legislation, including the Data Protection Act, information obtained about a participant during an investigation is confidential unless otherwise agreed in advance. Participants in psychological research have a right to expect that information they provide will be treated confidentially and, if published, will not be identifiable as theirs.

Protection of participants

Investigators have a responsibility to protect participants from physical and mental harm during the investigation. Normally, the risk of harm must be no greater than in ordinary life, i.e. participants should not be exposed to risks greater than or additional to those encountered in their normal lifestyles. Where research may involve behaviour or experiences that participants may regard as personal and private, the participants must be protected from stress by all appropriate measures, including the assurance that answers to personal questions need not be given.

Observational research

Studies based upon observation must respect the privacy and psychological wellbeing of the individuals studied. Unless those observed give their consent to being observed, observational research is only acceptable in situations where those observed would expect to be observed by strangers.

Giving advice

If, in the normal course of psychological research, a participant solicits advice concerning educational, personality, behavioural or health issues, caution should be exercised. If the issue is serious and the investigator is not qualified to offer assistance, the appropriate source of professional advice should be recommended.

The dilemma of deception

It can be argued that if participants are not deceived about the true aims of a study, their behaviour is affected and thus does not reflect how they would really behave in their everyday lives (e.g. participants show the effects of demand characteristics).

The dilemma for researchers is to design and conduct research that accurately portrays human behaviour while at the same time ensuring that they do not breach the ethical guidelines. Researchers may solve this dilemma by undertaking a cost–benefit analysis of the research before they commence. However, trying to balance potential benefits against potential costs raises problems:

■ It is almost impossible to calculate the costs and benefits before a study, as the researchers cannot predict events accurately.
■ Even after a study it is difficult to calculate the costs and benefits, as this may depend on when and who makes the judgement. The value of some research may not become apparent immediately, and participants, and even other researchers, may judge the benefits and costs differently.
■ This approach may encourage researchers to ignore the rights of the individual participants on the grounds that 'many more people will benefit'.

Knowledge check 30

When do researchers debrief the participants?

Exam tip

Make sure you can describe the BPS ethical guidelines.

The dilemma of informed consent

All participants should be asked to give informed consent prior to taking part in research. However, in some situations where deception may be used, it is not possible to obtain fully informed consent from the participants of the study and psychologists propose the following alternatives.

Presumptive consent

When presumptive consent is gained, people who are members of the population who are to be studied are informed of the details of the study and asked whether, *if they were to participate*, they would consider the research acceptable. Note that these 'potential participants' do not comprise the actual sample of participants.

Prior general consent

This involves asking questions of people who have volunteered to participate, before they are selected to take part. For example:

- Would you mind being involved in a study in which you were deceived?
- Would you mind taking part in a study if you were not informed of its true objectives?
- Would you mind taking part in a study that might cause you some stress?

Participants who say they 'would not mind' may later be selected to participate and it is assumed they have agreed in principle to the conditions of the study.

Research methods and ethical issues

Each research method raises different ethical issues, as follows:

- **Laboratory experiment.** Even when told they have the right to withdraw, participants may feel reluctant to do so and may feel they should do things they would not normally do. Participants may be deceived.
- **Field experiment.** It may be difficult to obtain informed consent and participants may not be able to withdraw. It may be difficult to debrief the participants.
- **Natural experiment.** Confidentiality may be a problem, as the sample studied may be identifiable. Where naturally occurring social variables are studied (e.g. family income, ethnicity), ethical issues may arise when drawing conclusions and publishing the findings.
- **Correlational studies.** Ethical issues can arise when researching relationships between socially sensitive variables (e.g. ethnicity and IQ) because published results can be misinterpreted as suggesting 'cause and effect'.
- **Naturalistic observations.** If informed consent is not being gained, people should only be observed in public places and where they would not be distressed to find they were being observed. If the location in which behaviour was observed is identifiable, an ethical issue may arise in terms of protecting confidentiality.
- **Interviews and questionnaires.** Participants should not be asked embarrassing questions (protection from psychological harm) and should be reminded that they do not have to answer any questions if they do not wish to. Protecting confidentiality is important.

Exam tip

Make sure you know the difference between failure to gain informed consent, and deception of participants.

Knowledge check 31

A student investigating the relationship between the type of attachment and the quality of young adult relationships designed a questionnaire and circulated it to all the students in her sixth form. Identify one ethical issue the researcher would need to consider.

Aims and hypotheses

The **research aim** is a general statement of the purpose of the study and should make clear what the study intends to investigate. The aim states the purpose of the study but is not precise enough to test.

A **hypothesis** states precisely what the researcher believes to be true about the target population. It is often generated from a theory and is a testable statement.

Experimental and alternative hypotheses

The term **experimental hypothesis** is used when experimental research is being conducted (laboratory, field or natural experiments); otherwise the term **alternative hypothesis** is used. The experimental hypothesis states that some difference (or effect) will occur; that the IV will have a significant effect on the DV.

The null hypothesis

The **null hypothesis** is a statement of no difference or of no correlation — the IV does not affect the DV — and is tested by the **inferential statistical test** (see p. 74).

If data analysis forces researchers to reject the null hypothesis, because a significant effect is found, they then accept the experimental hypothesis.

Directional and non-directional hypotheses

The experimental hypothesis can be directional or non-directional.

A **directional hypothesis** is termed a 'one-tailed hypothesis' because it predicts the direction in which the results are expected to go. Directional hypotheses are used when previous research evidence suggests that it is possible to make a clear prediction about the way in which the IV will affect the DV.

A **non-directional hypothesis** is termed a 'two-tailed hypothesis' because, although researchers expect that the IV will affect the DV, they are not sure how.

Sampling

When researchers conduct research, the **target population** is the group of people to whom they wish to generalise their findings. The **sample** of participants is the group of people who take part in the study, and a **representative sample** is a sample of people who are representative of the target population. There are several ways in which researchers select a sample.

Random sampling

This involves having the names of the target population and giving everyone an equal chance of being selected. A random sample can be selected by a computer or, in a small population, by selecting names from a hat.

Knowledge check 32

Loftus and Palmer carried out two experiments into the effect of leading questions on eyewitness testimony. Write an operationalised null hypothesis for the first experiment.

Exam tip

In the exam, when asked to write a hypothesis, students frequently confuse the null hypothesis with the alternative hypothesis. Practise writing alternative and null hypotheses.

Knowledge check 33

Loftus and Palmer carried out two experiments into the effect of leading questions on eyewitness testimony. Write a one-tailed (directional) experimental hypothesis for the second experiment.

> ### Evaluation
>
> **Strength**
> - A true random sample avoids bias, as every member of the target population has an equal chance of being selected.
>
> **Weakness**
> - It is almost impossible to obtain a truly random sample because not all the names of the target population may be known.

Opportunity sampling

This involves asking whoever is available and willing to participate. An opportunity sample is not likely to be representative of any target population because it will probably comprise friends of the researcher, or students, or people in a specific workplace. The people approached will be those who are local and available. A sample of participants approached 'in the street' is *not* a random sample of the population of a town. In a random sample, all the people living in a town would have an equal opportunity to participate. In an opportunity sample, only the people present at the time the researcher was seeking participants would be able to participate.

> ### Evaluation
>
> **Strength**
> - The researchers can quickly and inexpensively acquire a sample, and face-to-face ethical briefings and debriefings can be undertaken.
>
> **Weakness**
> - Opportunity samples are almost always biased samples, as who participates is dependent on who is asked and who happens to be available at the time.

Exam tip

A sample of people who are approached in a street is not a random sample — do not make this mistake.

Knowledge check 34

Explain why an opportunity sample is almost always a biased sample.

Volunteer sampling

Volunteer samples mean exactly that: people who volunteer to participate. A volunteer sample may not be representative of the target population because there may be differences between the sort of people who volunteer and those who do not.

> ### Evaluation
>
> **Strength**
> - The participants should have given their informed consent, will be interested in the research and may be less likely to withdraw.
>
> **Weakness**
> - A volunteer sample may be a biased sample that is not representative of the target population because volunteers may be different in some way from non-volunteers. For example, they may be more helpful (or more curious) than non-volunteers.

Systematic sampling

A systematic sample selects participants in a systematic way from the target population, for example, every tenth participant on a list of names. To take a systematic sample you list all the members of the population and then decide on a sample size. By dividing the number of people in the population by the number of people you want in your sample, you get a number and then you take every *n*th person to get a systematic sample.

Knowledge check 35

If you want a systematic sample of psychology students, and you need a sample of 20, from a list of 200 names which names will you pick?

Evaluation

Strength
- This method should provide a representative sample.

Weakness
- It is only possible if you can identify all members of the population to be studied.

Stratified sampling

In stratified sampling the researcher identifies the different types of people who make up the target population and works out the **proportions** needed for the sample to be representative.

A list is made of each variable of interest (e.g. IQ, gender, age group, occupation) which might have an effect on the research. For example, if we are interested in why or why not people participate in sporting activity, gender, age, and income may be important so we work out the relative percentage of each group in our population of interest. The sample must then contain all these groups in the same proportion as in the target population.

Evaluation

Strength
- The sample should be highly representative of the target population and therefore we can generalise from the results obtained.

Weakness
- Gathering such a sample would be time consuming and difficult to do and so this method is rarely used.

Sample representativeness

Researchers wish to apply the findings of their research to explain something about the behaviour of the target population; thus the sample of participants should be a true representation of diversity in the target population. In psychological research, students are often used as participants, but an all-student sample is only representative of a target population of students. Likewise, an all-male sample may only be representative of an all-male target population. If the sample is not representative, the research findings cannot be generalised to the target population.

Researchers also need to decide how many participants are needed, and the number required depends on several factors:

- The sample must be large enough to be representative of the target population.
- If the target population is small, then it may be possible, and sensible, to use the whole population as the sample. However, there is unlikely to be such a small target population in a psychology study.
- The sample needs to be of a manageable size, as too many participants make research expensive and time consuming.
- If the research has important implications (e.g. testing a new drug), the sample size should be larger than it would be in a less important study. In small samples, the individual differences between participants will have a greater effect. If the effect being studied is likely to be small, a larger sample will be required.

Pilot studies

A pilot study is an initial run-through of the procedures to be used in the research and usually involves selecting a few people and trying out the study on them. Pilot studies save time, and in some cases, money, by identifying any flaws in the procedures. A pilot study can help the researcher spot any unusual things or confusion in the information given to participants or problems with the task devised. For example, the procedure (task) may be too difficult and the researcher may get a floor effect, because none of the participants can complete the task, or the task may be too easy so that all participants achieve high scores and thus a ceiling effect occurs. A pilot study is particularly useful when a questionnaire is to be used, as the pilot study can help to identify any potential misunderstanding of the questions.

Experimental designs

Independent groups

Different participants are used in each of the conditions.

Evaluation

Strength
- No participants are 'lost' between trials. Participants can be randomly allocated between the conditions to distribute individual differences evenly. There are no practice effects.

Weakness
- It needs more participants and there may be important differences between the groups to start with that are not removed by the random allocation of participants between conditions.

Repeated measures

The same group of participants is used in each of the conditions.

Evaluation

Strength

- It requires fewer participants and controls for individual differences between participants as, in effect, the participants are compared against themselves.

Weakness

- It cannot be used in studies in which participation in one condition will affect responses in another (e.g. where participants learn tasks). It also cannot be used in studies where an order effect would create a problem (see below).

Knowledge check 36

Explain the difference between an independent design and a repeated measures design.
....

Order effects and counterbalancing

When a repeated measures design is used, problems may arise from participants doing the same task twice. The second time they carry out the task, they may be better than the first time because they have had practice, or worse than the first time because they have lost interest or are tired. If this happens, then an **order effect** is occurring.

One way that researchers control for order effects is to use a **counterbalancing technique**. The group of participants is split and half the group complete condition A followed by condition B; the other half completes condition B followed by condition A. In this way, any order effects are balanced out.

Matched pairs (matched participants) design

Separate groups of participants are used who are matched on a one-to-one basis on characteristics such as age or sex, to control for the possible effect of individual differences.

Evaluation

Strength

- Matching participants controls for some individual differences. It can be used when a repeated measures design is not appropriate (e.g. when performing the task twice would result in a practice effect).

Weakness

- A large number of prospective participants is often needed, from which to select matched pairs. It is difficult to match on some characteristics (e.g. personality).

Exam tip

You should be able to explain the advantages and disadvantages of the different experimental designs.
....

Observational design

Behavioural categories

When designing an observation the researcher must decide how different behaviour should be categorised in order to measure causes and effects. Some types of behaviour are relatively easy to categorise, e.g. 'walk', 'run', 'sleep', 'smoke', but others are more subtle. The strange situation (Ainsworth and Bell 1970) is an example of how infant behaviour has been categorised so that observers can identify types of attachment. Unless behaviour is clearly categorised different observers may interpret the same behaviour in different ways, resulting in low inter-observer reliability. When planning an observational study, the formulation of the hypothesis and decisions about how best to categorise the behaviour should be undertaken while carrying out preliminary observations of a small sample of participants.

Sampling behaviour

Once the behavioural categories have been decided, researchers need to decide who is going to be observed, how and when, and how the categories of behaviour are to be collected.

- **Focal sampling** records the behaviour of one individual at a time. For instance, you might decide to use focal sampling to observe the behaviour of a particular child in a playground, to record all the categories of aggressive incidents during a specified time period. One disadvantage of this method is that your focal 'person' may not engage in any of the behaviour categories of interest. Also, the person you are observing may become aware of your interest.
- **Event sampling** consists of observing a group and recording each time a specific behaviour (the event) occurs. This allows observation of a large number of individuals, but has the disadvantage that certain individuals or behaviour may be more conspicuous than others, leading to biased recording.
- **Time sampling** divides the observation period up into sample intervals, e.g. every 2 minutes. A watch can be used to indicate each sample interval. The observer makes a note of the behaviour occurring at each time interval on a pre-prepared tally chart. Bandura's Bobo doll study used a time sampling technique.

> **Knowledge check 37**
>
> You are going to conduct an observation of how students use their mobile phones. List two categories of behaviour you might observe.

Questionnaire construction

Questionnaires provide a relatively cheap, quick and efficient way of obtaining large amounts of information from a large sample of people. The language of a questionnaire should be appropriate to the vocabulary of the group of people being studied. Often a questionnaire uses both open and closed questions to collect data, which means that both quantitative and qualitative data can be obtained.

When designing a questionnaire researchers should make sure that any questions asked address the aims of the research. The longer the questionnaire is, the less likely people are to complete it. Questionnaires should be short, clear and to the point. A pilot study can be used to ensure people understand the questions. On the questionnaire, easier questions should be first, followed by more difficult questions. There should be a minimum of technical jargon.

Closed questions

Closed questions allow only answers which fit into categories that have been decided in advanced by the researcher, e.g. the answer can be yes or no, or answer options can be restricted to a list of alternatives from which the respondents can choose. Closed questions can also be rating scales — this often involves the participants choosing where on the scale best reflects their attitude.

Evaluation

Strength
- The data can be obtained quickly as closed questions are easy to answer. The questions are standardised — all respondents are asked the same questions in the same order which means the questionnaire can be replicated to check for reliability.

Weakness
- The answers lack detail — they tell the researcher 'what' but not 'why'.

Open questions

Open questions enable respondents to answer in as much detail as they like and provide qualitative information. However, they are harder to analyse and make comparisons from. Open questions are often used for questions that cannot be answered in a 'tick box' approach but require more detail and discussion.

Evaluation

Strength
- Rich qualitative data are obtained as open questions allow the respondents to elaborate and explain their answers.

Weakness
- It takes longer for the researchers to analyse qualitative data as they have to read the answers and try to put them into categories by coding, which is often subjective and difficult. Open questions may be problematic for less educated respondents as they require superior writing skills and an ability to express feelings verbally.

Design of interviews

Interviews are different from questionnaires as they involve social interaction. Researchers can ask closed questions or open questions that allow people to express what they think. Researchers use an interview schedule which is a set of prepared questions in a standardised format. This means the same questions are asked to each interviewee in the same order. The language the interviewer uses should be appropriate to the group of people being studied and interviews may not be the best method to use for researching socially sensitive topics. The researcher must decide whether to use a structured or non-structured interview and must consider who the interviewer will be. There are a number of variables to consider:

- The gender and age of the interviewer can have a big effect on respondents' answers, particularly on personal issues.
- The personal characteristics, accent, and appearance of the interviewer can also have an effect.
- The ethnicity of the interviewer, as people can have difficulty interviewing respondents from a different ethnic group.

Structured interviews

The questions are asked in a set/standardised order and the interviewer will not deviate from the interview schedule.

Evaluation

Strength

- Structured interviews are easy to replicate as a fixed set of closed questions are used. This also means it is easy to test for reliability. Structured interviews are fairly quick to conduct which means that many interviews can take place within a short amount of time.

Weakness

- Structured interviews are not flexible so new questions cannot be asked during the interview.

Unstructured interviews

These are sometimes referred to as **discovery interviews** and they contain open-ended questions that can be asked in any order.

Evaluation

Strength

- These are more flexible as questions can be adapted and changed depending on the respondents' answers. They generate qualitative data through the use of open questions which allow the respondent to talk in depth so the researcher develops a sense of a person's understanding of a situation. They have increased validity because it gives the interviewer the opportunity to ask for clarification and allows the interviewee to steer the direction of the interview etc.

Weakness

- They can be time consuming to conduct and to analyse the qualitative data. Training interviewers is expensive and skills may be needed by the interviewer, for example the ability to establish a rapport with the respondent.

Knowledge check 38

In a questionnaire and/ or interview, what types of data are collected by an open question?

Exam tip

Be prepared to answer an exam question on the difference between a structured and unstructured interview.

Variables and control
Variables

- **Independent variable (IV).** The IV is the variable we manipulate in experimental research.
- **Dependent variable (DV).** The dependent variable is the variable we measure in experimental research.
- **Operationalisation of variables.** Operationalisation means being able to define variables in order to manipulate the IV and measure the DV. However, some variables are easier to operationalise than others. For example, performance on a memory test might be operationalised as 'the number of words remembered', but it is more difficult to operationalise how stressed someone may be. You could operationalise stress by measuring physiological arousal, or you could ask participants to rate how stressed they were. Both the IV and the DV need to be precisely operationalised otherwise the research cannot be replicated because another researcher would not be able to set up a study to repeat the same measurements.
- **Control of extraneous variables.** Any variables that change between the conditions, other than the IV, are difficult to control (e.g. how tired the participants are). Environmental variables that may affect participants' performance, such as the time of day or location, also need to be controlled.
- **Extraneous or confounding variables.** These include any variables that have not been controlled and that may also have an effect in the IV or on the DV which reduces the experimental validity of the study. Extraneous variables are variables that change between the conditions, other than the IV, and are difficult to control (e.g. how tired the participants are). Confounding variables may be environmental variables that may affect participants' performance, such as the time of day or location. These also need to be controlled.

Knowledge check 39

How did Milgram operationalise obedience?

Exam tip

In an exam you may be given an outline of a hypothetical research study and asked to suggest which extraneous variables you would control and why these variables should be controlled.

Control

Controls should be used to try to avoid variables other than the IV from affecting the DV. Controls can include **random allocation** of participants to experimental conditions to distribute individual differences within the sample equally between conditions. Controls can also include **counterbalancing** (see repeated measures on page 57) and **standardisation**, such as the use of standardised instructions and procedures by which all participants are told what to do in exactly the same way and are treated in exactly the same way. **Randomisation** can also be used, in which material for different experimental conditions is presented in random order to prevent order effects.

Demand characteristics and investigator effects

Demand characteristics

Regardless of other variables, as soon as people know their behaviour is of interest, it is likely to change. Some ways in which participation in research can affect behaviour are as follows:

- **The Hawthorne effect.** If people are aware that they are being studied, they are likely to try harder on tasks and pay more attention. This may mean that any findings (e.g. response times) are artificially high, which may lead to invalid conclusions.

■ **Demand characteristics.** Sometimes, features of the research situation, the research task and possibly the researcher may give cues to participants as to what is expected of them or how they are expected to behave, or in some way change participant behaviour. This may lead to response bias, in which participants try to please the experimenter (or deliberately do the opposite), in which case conclusions drawn from the findings may be invalid. Demand characteristics may be reduced if a **single-blind procedure** is used. Here, participants do not know which condition they are participating in, or are given a false account of the experiment. If a single-blind procedure is used, ethical issues arise because fully informed consent cannot be gained. However, if features of the research task cue participants to change their behaviour, a single-blind procedure will not control for this.

■ **Social desirability bias.** People usually try to show themselves in the best possible way. So, when answering questions in interviews or questionnaires, they may give answers that are socially acceptable but not truthful. For example, people tend to under-report anti-social behaviour, such as alcohol consumption and smoking, and over-report pro-social behaviour, such as giving to charity.

Knowledge check 40

A researcher circulated a questionnaire to parents asking them the following question: *Which of these best describes your child? My child behaves aggressively — Very often, Often, Rarely, Never.* Explain why this question may give rise to social desirability bias.

Investigator effects

An **investigator** is the person who designs the study and an **experimenter** is the person who conducts the study. They may or may not always be the same person. Researchers may unwittingly affect the results of their research in several ways:

■ **Investigator expectancy.** The expectations of the researcher can affect how they design their research and bias how and what they decide to measure, and how the findings are analysed.

■ **Experimenter bias.** The experimenter can affect the way participants behave. One way to reduce experimenter effects is to use a **double-blind procedure** in which neither the experimenter nor the participants know what the research hypothesis is.

■ **Interviewer effects.** The expectations of the interviewer may lead them to ask only those questions in which they are interested, or to ask leading questions, or they may only focus on answers that match their expectations.

■ **Observer bias.** When observing behaviour, observers may make biased interpretations of the meaning of behaviour.

The role of peer review in the scientific process

Peers are professionals in the same field as the psychologist whose research is being reviewed and the most common way of validating new knowledge is peer review. Peer reviews serve three main purposes:

■ **Allocation of research funding.** The peer reviews help to determine where research funding should go.

■ **Publication in scientific journals.** Peer reviews help decide whether research is good enough to be published and positive peer reviews can catch the eye of journal editors.

■ **Research rating of a university department.** A positive peer review can improve the research rating and credibility of a university/department.

The internet and peer review. More research is being published in internet-based journals and the nature of peer review is changing. Usually, peers are experts in the research field but any reader can review research published on the internet.

Knowledge check 41

Suggest two ways that peer review is useful.

Reliability and types of validity

This topic is not examined on AS papers.

Reliability

Reliability of results means consistency. In other words, if something is measured more than once, the same effect should result. If my tape measure tells me I am 152 cm tall one day but 182 cm tall the next, the tape measure I am using is not reliable.

Internal reliability refers to how consistently a method measures within itself. For example, my tape measure should measure the same distance between 0 cm and 10 cm as it does between 10 cm and 20 cm. To test for internal reliability, researchers may use the **split-half technique** in which half of the scores are compared with the other half to see how similar they are.

External reliability refers to the consistency of measures over time (i.e. if repeated). For example, personality tests should not give different results if the same person is tested more than once. External reliability can be tested by the **test–retest method**. For example, the same participants can be tested on more than one occasion to see whether their results remain similar.

Inter-observer reliability assesses whether, in an observational study, if several observers are coding behaviour, their codings or ratings agree with each other. To **improve reliability**, all observers must have clear and operationalised categories of behaviour and must be trained in how to use the system. Inter-observer reliability can be measured using correlational analysis, in which a high positive correlation among ratings indicates that high inter-observer reliability has been established.

Types of validity

Internal validity refers to the extent to which a measurement technique measures what it is supposed to measure, whether the IV really caused the effect on the DV or whether some other factor was responsible. Experiments may lack internal validity because of demand characteristics or participant reactivity, or because extraneous variables have not been controlled. Internal validity can be improved by controlling extraneous variables, using standardised instructions, counterbalancing, and eliminating demand characteristics and investigator effects.

Another aspect of internal validity is **mundane realism**, i.e. do the measures used generalise to real life? For example, does a measure of long-term memory based on remembering lists of words generalise to how people really remember past events? Mundane realism is an aspect of internal validity that contributes to external validity.

External validity refers to the validity of a study outside the research situation and provides some idea of the extent to which the findings can be generalised. To assess the external validity of research, three factors should be considered:

- How representative is the sample of participants of the population to which the results are to be generalised (**population validity**)?
- Do the research setting and situation generalise to a realistic real-life setting or situation (**ecological validity**)?
- Do the findings generalise to the past and to the future (**temporal validity**)? For example, it is argued that 50 years ago people were more conformist and obedient.

Face validity is simply whether the test appears, at face value, to measure what it claims to.

Construct validity refers to the extent to which a test captures a specific construct or trait, and it overlaps with some of the other aspects of validity. To test for construct validity it must be demonstrated that the phenomenon being measured actually exists. So, the construct validity of a test for intelligence is dependent on a model or theory of intelligence.

Concurrent validity is the degree to which a test corresponds to an external criterion that is known concurrently (i.e. occurring at the same time). If the new test is validated by a comparison with a currently existing criterion, we have concurrent validity.

Features of science

This topic is not examined on AS papers.

The scientific approach is empirical (i.e. all knowledge comes through our senses). The nature of scientific enquiry may be thought of as to do with theory and the foundation of hypotheses and with empirical methods of enquiry (i.e. experiments, observations). The most empirical method of enquiry in science is the experiment. The important features of the experiment are control over variables (independent, dependent and extraneous), careful objective measurement and establishing cause and effect relationships.

Key features of science include:
- **Empirical evidence.** Data are collected through direct observation or experiment. Empirical evidence does not rely on argument or belief. Experiments and observations are carried out carefully and reported in detail so that other investigators can repeat and attempt to verify the work.
- **Objectivity.** Researchers remain unbiased in their investigations and all sources of bias such as personal or subjective ideas are eliminated.
- **Control.** Extraneous variables need to be controlled in order to be able to establish cause (IV) and effect (DV).
- **Predictability.** Scientists should aim to be able to predict future behaviour from the findings of research.
- **Hypothesis testing.** A hypothesis serves as a prediction and is derived from a theory. Hypotheses need to be stated in a form that can be tested (i.e. operationalised and unambiguous).
- **Replication.** Can a particular method and finding be repeated with different/same people and/or on different occasions, to see if the results are the same? If a discovery is reported but it cannot be replicated by other scientists it will not be accepted. Replicability of research is vital in establishing a scientific theory.

Knowledge check 42

Suggest two ways that the internal validity of research may be reduced.

Exam tip

Make sure you know the difference between research reliability and research validity.

Is psychology a science?

Thomas Kuhn argues that scientific disciplines have one predominant **paradigm** that almost all scientists subscribe to and that anything with several paradigms (e.g. models, theories) is not a science until the multiple theories are unified. Because psychologists do not have any universal laws of human behaviour, and since there are many paradigms (approaches) within psychology, Kuhn would argue that psychology is not a science.

According to Kuhn, a **paradigm shift** is a change in the basic assumptions, or paradigms, within the ruling theory of a science. Kuhn believed that, 'a student in the humanities (e.g. psychology), has constantly before him a number of competing solutions to problems' (think of the different approaches to explaining behaviour as being the competing explanations). Kuhn argues that once a paradigm shift is complete, a scientist (e.g. a physicist or chemist) cannot reject the new theory (paradigm), but in psychology researchers can choose to adopt an array of stances (e.g. cognitive, behaviourist, biological, and psychodynamic explanations for human behaviour).

Reporting psychological investigations

This topic is not examined on AS papers.

Psychological reports are always presented in the same research report structure.

Sections of a scientific report

Title page: This indicates what the study is about — the research question.

Abstract: The abstract allows the readers to find out the essentials of the research before they read the detail of research. The abstract gives brief details of the topic of the study, the participants — who, when, where, how many; the method, design, the experimental task, questionnaires etc. It also includes the major findings and the conclusion drawn from them and implications for further research.

Introduction: The introduction explains the background to the research hypothesis and outlines specific and relevant background research. The introduction includes the aim of the research and the hypotheses to be tested.

Method: The method is written in detail so that the research can be replicated. It includes details on:
- **Experimental design:** (if appropriate) independent and dependent variables, what participants had to do, what was controlled and how.
- **Participants:** the target population, how the sample was obtained, why this sample was chosen, and details such as age range and gender of the sample.
- **Materials:** the materials used, e.g. pictures, word lists, instructions, debrief, record sheets etc. Examples of the actual materials are included in the appendix to the report.
- **Procedure:** the precise procedure followed, including detail on the brief, standardised instructions and debriefing.

Knowledge check 43

Explain why Kuhn would argue that psychology is not a science.

Exam tip

Be prepared to answer an exam question on whether psychology can be seen as a science.

Content Guidance

Results: A summary of the findings, including statistics, tables and/or charts and, if appropriate, the inferential statistical tests used and why these tests were chosen, the observed and critical values of the tests and the research conclusion in terms of the hypothesis.

Discussion: The discussion section compares the results to background materials from the introduction section and talks about whether/why similarities or differences have been found. The discussion section also contains a critique of the research and ideas for further research.

References: In this section all the books and materials referred to in the course of the research are cited. In psychological reports, references are always set out in APA referencing format. References must be listed in alphabetical order of surname.

(APA referencing guidelines are laid out in the sixth edition of the *Publication Manual of the American Psychological Association*.)

Knowledge check 44

List the elements that make up a published psychological report.

Exam tip

Practise writing references in the APA format — in the exam you may be given an example of a wrongly written reference and asked to correct it.

Knowledge summary

At AS and A-level you should be able to identify and describe/explain:

- the British Psychological Society (BPS) code of ethics and recognise ethical issues and the ways in which psychologists deal with them
- aims and hypotheses, including directional and non-directional hypotheses
- sampling techniques, including random, opportunity and volunteer sampling
- the need for pilot studies
- experimental design (independent groups, repeated measures and matched pairs)
- design of naturalistic observations, including the development and use of behavioural categories
- design of questionnaires and interviews
- operationalisation of variables, including independent and dependent, and control of extraneous variables
- the use of controls
- demand characteristics and ways in which an investigator may affect research
- the role of peer review in the scientific process

At A-level you should also be able to:

- define reliability and validity and differentiate between these
- explain the key features of the scientific approach
- describe the structure of psychological reports

■Data handling and analysis

You must be familiar with ways that quantitative and qualitative data can be analysed, presented and interpreted.

Quantitative and qualitative data

Experimental research, observations, interviews and questionnaires can result in **quantitative** and/or **qualitative data**.

Exam tip

You should be able to explain why the strange situation collects qualitative data.

Evaluation

Strengths of quantitative data
- They are objective.
- Precise measures are used.
- Data are high in reliability.
- It is possible to see patterns in the data.

Weaknesses of quantitative data
- They may lack or lose detail.
- They are often collected in contrived settings.

Strengths of qualitative data
- They are rich and detailed.
- They are collected in real-life settings.
- They can provide information on people's attitudes, opinions and beliefs.

Weaknesses of qualitative data
- They may be subjective.
- They can be an imprecise measure.
- They may be low in reliability.

Primary and secondary data

Primary data are collected by a range of different methods, including observation, surveys, interviews, experiments and case studies. Primary data are more reliable than secondary data because the researcher knows the sources.

Secondary data are data collected from external sources. These methods can include television, radio, internet, magazines, newspapers, reviews, research articles, and stories told by others. However, with secondary data, issues such as validity and reliability occur as the researcher is less sure of the accuracy of the source.

Meta-analysis is a statistical technique that involves combining and analysing the results of different individual studies on a specific topic. This technique allows researchers to identify any trends and relationships that might exist. Because a meta-analysis combines multiple smaller samples into a much larger pool of data, researchers can sometimes identify trends that would not be seen in smaller-scale studies.

Descriptive statistics

Measures of **central tendency** and **dispersion** are used to summarise large amounts of data into typical or average values, and to provide information on the variability or spread of the scores.

Measures of central tendency

There are three ways to calculate the average of a set of scores: the mean, the median and the mode.

The mean

To calculate the **mean**, all the scores are added up and the total is divided by the number of the scores.

For example, take the following set of scores: 1, 2, 3, 3, 4, 5, 5, 7, 8, 9.

The mean of this set of scores is 4.7 (47/10).

> ### Evaluation
>
> #### Strength
> ● It takes all the values from the raw scores into account.
>
> #### Weaknesses
> ● The mean can give a distorted impression if there are unusual (extremely high or low) scores in the data set.
> ● Often, the mean may have a 'meaningless' decimal point that was not in the original scores (e.g. 2.4 children).

The median

The **median** is the central score in a list of rank-ordered scores. In an odd number of scores, the median is the middle number. In an even-numbered set of scores, the median is the midpoint between the two middle scores.

For example, take the following set of scores: 2, 3, 4, 5, 5, 6, 7, 8, 15, 16.

The median of this set of scores is (5 + 6)/2 = 5.5.

The mean of this set of scores is 7.1 (71/10).

> ### Evaluation
>
> #### Strengths
> ● The median is not affected by extreme scores.
> ● It is useful when scores are ordered data (first, second, third etc.)
>
> #### Weaknesses
> ● The median does not take account of the values of all of the scores.
> ● It can be misleading if used in small sets of scores.

> **Exam tip**
>
> Make sure you know the difference between the measures of central tendency: mean, median and mode.

The mode

The **mode** is the score that occurs most frequently in a set of scores.

For example, take the following set of scores: 4, 4, 4, 4, 5, 6, 10, 12, 12, 14.

The mode of this set of scores is 4 because it occurs four times (the most frequently).

The median of this set of scores is (5 + 6)/2 = 5.5. The mean is 7.5 (75/10). This example shows that each of the measures of central tendency may describe the midpoint of a set of scores differently.

Knowledge check 45

Explain one disadvantage of using the mean as a measure of central tendency of a small sample of scores.

Evaluation

Strengths
- The mode is not affected by extreme scores.
- It is useful when nominal level (frequency level) data are collected.

Weaknesses
- The mode tells us nothing about other scores.
- There may be more than one mode in a set of data.

NB **Nominal level data** means that the frequency of instances can only be counted, e.g. 2 red cars, 3 blue cars, 4 silver cars. The data cannot be put into rank order, e.g. because a red car is not more of anything than a blue car.

Measures of dispersion

Measures of dispersion tell us about how far spread out the data are. The main measures of dispersion are the range and the standard deviation.

Range

To calculate the **range** of a set of scores, subtract the lowest score from the highest score. For example, the range of a set of scores having a lowest score of 10 and a highest score of 24 is 14. The range is a useful measure because if our research has more than one condition, we can compare the range of the scores obtained in each condition. A low range indicates consistency in participant scores and thus low levels of individual differences. A high range indicates variation in participant scores and thus high levels of participant differences. (Note that 'low' or 'high' is relative to the maximum possible range of scores.)

Evaluation

Strengths
- It is easy and quick to work out.
- It includes extreme values.

Weakness
- It may be misleading when there are extremely high or low scores in a set.

Standard deviation

Standard deviation is used to measure how the scores are distributed around the central point (the mean). The greater the standard deviation, the larger the spread of the scores. Standard deviation is useful because when scores are 'normally distributed', about 68% of the scores will lie within 1 standard deviations above or below the mean (see also normal distributions on page 72).

Knowledge check 46

What is the difference between a measure of central tendency and a measure of dispersion?

Evaluation

Strengths
- Standard deviation allows for an interpretation of any individual score in a set, and is particularly useful in large sets of scores.
- It is a sensitive measure of dispersion because all the scores are used in its calculation.

Weaknesses
- Standard deviation is not useful when data are not normally distributed.
- It is quite complicated to calculate.

Exam tip

You need to know the difference between measures of central tendency and measures of dispersion. Practise using these and explaining how they are used.

Presentation and display of quantitative data

Psychologists use graphs and charts to summarise their data in visual displays. Information provided in graphs and charts makes it easier for others to understand the findings of research.

Bar charts

Bar charts are used when scores are in categories, when there is no fixed order for the items on the *x*-axis; or they can be used to show a comparison of means for continuous data. This bar chart shows the holiday destinations chosen by a sample of 300 families. The bars in bar charts should be the same width but should not touch. The space between the bars illustrates that the variable on the *y*-axis consists of discrete data.

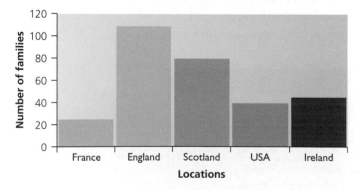

Figure 8 Bar chart showing holiday destinations

Histograms

Histograms are not examined at AS.

Histograms show frequencies of scores (how the scores are distributed) using columns. They should be used to display frequency distributions of continuous data and there should be no gaps between the bars. This example shows the exam results (marks) for a class of 30 students in a mock exam marked out of a maximum of 100. The scores have been grouped into ranges of 10 marks.

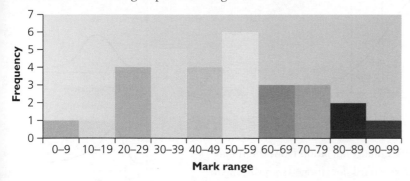

Figure 9 Histogram showing distribution of marks in a mock exam

Scattergrams

Scattergrams are used to depict the result of **correlational analysis**. A scattergram shows at a glance whether there appears to be a **positive** or **negative correlation**, or **no correlation**.

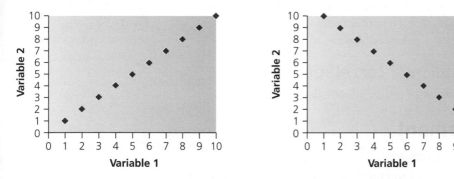

Figure 10 Scattergrams showing positive and negative correlations between two variables

Tables

Psychologists present the findings of research in tables to make it easy for others to see and interpret the results at a glance.

Example

Correct answers in a maths test	Condition A male	Condition B female
Mean	12.11	15.23
Median	11	14
Range	6	4
Standard deviation	2.25	3.5

Distributions and correlation

Normal distributions

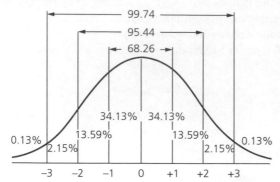

Figure 11 The U-shaped curve of normal distribution

Exam tip
You need to be able to explain what is meant by normal distribution.

In a normally distributed set of scores:

- 68.26% of the scores lie within +1 or −1 standard deviation from the mean
- 95.44% of the scores lie within +2 or −2 standard deviations from the mean
- 99.74% of scores lie within +3 or −3 standard deviations from the mean

Thus in a normally distributed set of scores only 4.56% of the scores will lie more than +2, or −2 standard deviations above or below the mean.

Skewed distributions

However, sometimes the sample size may be so small that it is difficult to know whether the data are normally distributed. Sometimes data are not normally distributed (see Figure 12) and there is a **skewed distribution**.

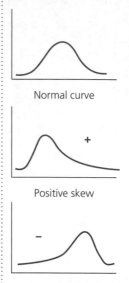

Figure 12 Normal and skewed distributions

Analysis and interpretation of correlation

Refer to earlier section on 'Correlations' in research methods (see page 47).

Levels of measurement

This topic is not examined on AS papers.

- **Nominal level data (frequencies of occurrence).** *Examples:* How many cars are red, green or blue; how many people are left or right handed. Use the **mode** as the measure of central tendency. It makes no sense to calculate the mean because you can't actually have 2.4 children or the average of 5 red cars and 2 yellow cars.
- **Ordinal level data — can be ranked in order: 1st, 2nd, 3rd etc.** *Example:* Scores = 1, 3, 4, 6, 8, 9, 11, 15, 50. Use the **median** as the measure of central tendency (middle score) because the mean can be affected by 'extreme' scores.
- **Interval level data — measured on a fixed scale, e.g. height in inches, weight in grams.** *Example:* Temperature = 13.1, 15.2, 16.2, 17.2, 18.2, 19.5. Use the **mean** as the measure of central tendency (mathematical midpoint) because this gives a precise measure of the central tendency – but remember that the mean can be affected by 'extreme' scores.

Content analysis and coding

This topic is not examined on AS papers.

Analysing and coding qualitative data

In interviews and observations, qualitative data might result from video or audio recordings or written notes. Likewise, qualitative data can result when open questions are asked in interviews or questionnaires, or when participants are invited to explain why they behave in a certain way. It is important when analysing qualitative data that researchers avoid subjective or biased misinterpretations. Misinterpretation can be avoided by:

- using accurate language to operationalise the variables to be measured — e.g. if observing play-fighting in children, an operationalised definition might be 'hitting while smiling' (though counting the frequency would be quantitative data)
- using a team of observers who have verified their inter-observer reliability
- converting qualitative data into quantitative data; one way is by coding the data

When a sample of qualitative data has been collected — for example, from the interviewee, from magazines or newspapers, or from the notes or recordings of an observation, **coding units** are identified in order to categorise the data. A coding unit could be specific words or phrases that are looked for (the operationalised definitions). The coding units may then be counted to see how frequently they occur. The resulting frequency of occurrence is a form of quantitative data.

Thematic analysis

Thematic analysis is used in qualitative research. It emphasises pinpointing, examining and recording patterns (or themes) within data. Themes are patterns across data sets that are important to the description of a phenomenon and are associated with a specific research question. The themes become the categories for analysis. Thematic analysis is performed through the process of coding in **six phases** to create established, meaningful patterns. These phases are: (1) familiarisation with data, (2) generating initial codes, (3) searching for themes among codes, (4) reviewing themes, (5) defining and naming themes, and (6) producing the final report.

> **Knowledge check 47**
>
> You are carrying out a content analysis of the language used in television advertisements for food. Suggest two categories that could be used in this content analysis.

Knowledge summary

At AS and A-level you should be able to:
- define quantitative and qualitative data and differentiate between these
- explain the difference between primary and secondary data
- calculate measures of central tendency including median, mean, mode and know when to use these
- calculate measures of dispersion including ranges and standard deviation and be able to explain why dispersions are useful
- present quantitative data in visual diagrams including bar charts, scattergrams and tables

- explain normal and skewed distributions

At A-level you should also be able to:
- present quantitative data on histograms
- analyse and interpret correlational data and differentiate between positive and negative correlations
- know what is meant by a correlation coefficient and how to interpret these
- describe ways of analysing qualitative data and the processes involved in content analysis

Inferential testing

Introduction to statistical tests

An inferential statistical test is a way of analysing the findings of a study and 'inferring' characteristics from a small sample of people to apply to much larger groups of people (the population). In the A-level exam you may be asked to identify when to use which inferential statistical test and you need to be able to explain why you selected the test you suggest. You need to be able to demonstrate knowledge and understanding of how and why inferential tests are used and be familiar with their use, and you must be able to respond to questions on probability and significance.

A **statistically significant result** is one which is unlikely to have occurred by chance. When a result is unlikely to have occurred by chance then researchers will reject the null hypothesis and retain the alternative hypothesis. Using inferential statistical tests allows psychologists to find out whether their findings are significant. Many inferential statistical tests require that data follow a **normal distribution** (see page 72). In cases where data follow a skewed distribution it is necessary to use a **non-parametric test** that does not require the data to be normally distributed.

The sign test

The sign test is a **non-parametric** inferential test of difference that is suitable for use with related data. The sign test examines the direction of difference between pairs of scores from the same participants in a repeated measures design experiment (see page 57).

Example

A psychologist wanted to find out whether watching a documentary about older people playing sport changed student attitudes towards older people. A sample of students was used and a base line measure of attitudes was taken using a rating scale question where 0 = very unfavourable and 10 = very favourable. The students then watched a 20-minute documentary after which they were asked the same attitude question. A table of results was constructed.

Participant	Attitude	Direction of difference
1	More favourable	+
2	More favourable	+
3	No change	Omitted
4	Less favourable	−
5	More favourable	+
6	More favourable	+

In the results four of the six participants reported more favourable attitudes. However, as an inferential test the sign test is not a very powerful test as it only takes into consideration the direction of the differences rather than the value of any differences.

Knowledge check 48

Is the sign test used to analyse the data from independent or repeated measures design?

Which inferential test to use?

This topic is not examined on AS papers.

- **The Mann–Whitney U-test is a non-parametric test.** It is a test of the significance of the difference between two conditions. It is suitable for use when an independent design has been used **and** the level of data collected is 'at least' ordinal.
- **The unrelated t-test is a parametric test.** It is a test of the significance of the difference between two conditions. It is suitable for use when an independent design has been used **and** the level of data collected is 'at least' ordinal **and** the data are normally distributed.
- **The Wilcoxon matched pairs signed ranks test is a non-parametric test.** It is a test of the significance of the difference between two conditions when a repeated measures design has been used **and** the level of data collected is 'at least' ordinal.
- **The related t-test is a parametric test.** It is a test of the significance of the difference between two conditions when a repeated measures design has been used **and** the level of data collected is 'at least' ordinal **and** the data are normally distributed.
- **The Spearman's rho** (rank order) correlation co-efficient is used when a correlation between two independent variables is being analysed. It is a **non-parametric test** which calculates the correlation coefficient between ranked scores when both sets of scores are 'at least' ordinal data (i.e. can be placed in rank order).
- **Pearson's r** correlation coefficient is used when a correlation between two independent variables is being analysed. It is a **parametric test** which calculates the correlation coefficient between actual scores that must be 'at least' ordinal.
- **The Chi-Squared test** is a test of significance of association. It is used when **nominal level data** (frequency data) have been collected.

Probability and significance

This topic is not examined on AS papers.

Critical values in interpretation of significance

For all of the different inferential tests, mathematicians have calculated the critical values for significance. When the inferential test has calculated the statistical result we can compare the result against the table of critical values. The table below shows critical values at different levels of significance for Spearman's rho. So for 10 pairs of scores, if a standard $p=<0.05$ is selected (probability less than 5% chance) the value of the calculated correlation coefficient must be equal to or greater than +/–0.5760 to be significant.

Exam tip

You may be given a hypothetical research study and asked to explain a choice of statistical test. If you selected a Mann–Whitney test, an appropriate explanation would be: 'I wanted to find out whether the difference between the two experimental groups is significant and for an independent design with ordinal level data the Mann–Whitney U-test is appropriate.'

Values of the correlation coefficient for different levels of significance for Spearman's rho

N	P = 0.1	P = 0.05	P = 0.02	P = 0.01
1	.99	.99	.99	.99
2	.90	.95	.98	.99
3	.81	.88	.93	.96
4	.73	.81	.88	.92
5	.67	.75	.83	.87
6	.62	.71	.79	.83
7	.58	.67	.75	.80
8	.55	.63	.72	.76
9	.52	.60	.69	.73
10	.48	.58	.66	.71

Type 1 and Type 2 errors

When psychologists decide whether to reject or retain the **null hypothesis** they look at the results of the statistical test. However, there is always the possibility that they may make an error:

- A **Type 1 error** is deciding to reject the null hypothesis, concluding that the IV did have a significant effect on the DV when actually the result was due to chance or some other factor.
- A **Type 2 error** is deciding to retain the null hypothesis, concluding that the IV had no significant effect on the DV when actually the result was caused by the IV.

The level of significance selected affects whether researchers are likely to make a Type 1 error or a Type 2 error. If researchers set the level of significance low at $p = <0.10$ they are more likely to make a Type 1 error. However, if researchers set the level of significance high, e.g. at $p = <0.001$ they are more likely to make a Type 2 error.

Knowledge check 49

What is meant by $p = <0.05$?

Exam tip

Be ready to explain the difference between making a Type 1 or Type 2 error.

Knowledge summary

At AS and A-level you should:
- be familiar with the concept of statistical testing, including the sign test

At A-level you should also be able to:
- demonstrate knowledge and understanding of inferential tests and be familiar with their use

- discuss factors affecting the choice of statistical test, including level of measurement and experimental design
- respond to questions on probability and significance, including the use of critical values and Type 1 and Type 2 errors

■ Research methods: glossary of terms

NB This section has been included here at the end of all the topics linked to research methods as many of the terms occur in more than one topic.

correlation: a statistical technique used to calculate the correlation coefficient in order to quantify the strength of relationship between two variables.

counterbalancing: a way of controlling for order effects by having half the participants complete condition A followed by condition B; the other participants complete condition B followed by condition A.

demand characteristics: aspects of the experiment may act as cues to behaviour that cause the participants (and the experimenter) to change the way they behave.

dependent variable (DV): the effect of the IV, or what is measured, in an experiment.

ethical guidelines: the British Psychological Society (BPS) has issued a set of ethical guidelines for research involving human participants. These ethical guidelines are designed to protect the wellbeing and dignity of research participants.

external validity: the validity of a study outside the research situation and the extent to which the findings can be generalised.

field experiment: a way of conducting research in an everyday environment, e.g. in a school or hospital, where one or more IVs are manipulated by the experimenter and the effect it may have (the DV) is measured.

Hawthorne effect: when people are aware that they are being studied, they are likely to try harder on tasks and pay more attention.

hypothesis: this states precisely what the researcher believes to be true about the target population and is a testable statement.

independent groups design: different participants are used in each of the conditions.

independent variable (IV): the variable that is manipulated (changed) between experimental conditions.

inferential statistical test: a way of analysing the findings of a study and 'inferring' characteristics from a small sample of people to apply to much larger groups of people (the population).

internal validity: the extent to which a measurement technique measures what it is supposed to measure, whether the IV really caused the effect on the DV or whether some other factor was responsible.

inter-observer reliability: whether, in an observational study, if several observers are coding behaviour, their codings or ratings agree with each other.

laboratory experiment: a method of conducting research in which researchers try to control all the variables except the one that is changed between the experimental conditions.

matched participants design: separate groups of participants are used who are matched on a one-to-one basis on characteristics such as age or sex, to control for the possible effect of individual differences.

natural experiment: an experimental method, in which, rather than being manipulated by the researcher, the IV to be studied is naturally occurring. Some examples of naturally occurring variables are gender and age.

naturalistic observations: a research method in which psychologists watch people's behaviour but remain inconspicuous and do nothing to change or interfere with it.

null hypothesis: a statement of no difference or of no correlation — the IV does not affect the DV. It is tested by the inferential statistical test.

operationalisation of variables: being able to define variables in order to manipulate the IV and measure the DV, e.g. performance on a memory test might be operationalised as 'the number of words remembered from a list of words'.

opportunity sampling: asking whoever is available and willing to participate. An opportunity sample is not likely to be representative of any target population because it will probably comprise friends of the researcher, or students, or people in a specific workplace.

order effects: when a repeated measures design is used, problems may arise from participants doing the same task twice because the second time they carry out the task, they may be better than the first time because they have had practice or worse than the first time because they have lost interest or are tired.

pilot studies: a trial run of research with a small number of participants for researchers to make necessary adjustments and to save wasting valuable resources.

qualitative data: rich and detailed data collected in real-life settings, for example people's subjective opinions.

quantitative data: objective, precise, usually numerical, data that can be statistically analysed.

random sampling: having the names of the target population and giving everyone an equal chance of being selected.

reliability: reliability of results means consistency. In other words, if something is measured more than once, the same effect should result.

repeated measures design: the same group of participants is used in each of the conditions.

research aim: a general statement of the purpose of the study. It should make clear what the study intends to investigate.

self-report method: a way of finding out about people's behaviour by interviewing them or by asking them to fill out questionnaires.

structured interviews: participants are asked the same questions in the same order.

social desirability bias: when people try to show themselves in the best possible way, so that when answering questions in interviews or questionnaires they give answers that are socially acceptable but are not truthful.

unstructured interviews: participants can discuss anything freely and the interviewer devises new questions on the basis of answers previously given.

volunteer sampling: participants volunteer to participate, e.g. by responding to advertisements.

Questions & Answers

This section contains 12 questions — four on approaches in psychology, five on biopsychology and three on research methods and data handling and analysis. Those questions which are on topics not examined at AS are clearly identified.

The section is structured as follows:

- sample questions in the style of the exam
- example student responses at grade A/B (student A), demonstrating thorough knowledge, good understanding and an ability to deal with the data presented in the question
- example student responses at grade C/D (student B), demonstrating strengths and weaknesses and the potential for improvement

All example responses are followed by exam advice, preceded by the icon **e**. This may indicate where credit is due, strengths in the answer, areas for improvement, specific problems, common errors, lack of clarity, irrelevance, mistakes in the meaning of terms and/or misinterpretation of the question. Comments indicate how the answers might be marked in an exam. Some questions are also followed by a brief analysis of what to watch out for when answering them (shown by the icon **e**).

Exam format

If you are studying A-level Psychology the examinations are all taken at the end of your 2-year course and the exams include synoptic questions to allow you to demonstrate your ability to draw together your skill, knowledge and understanding from across the full course and to provide extended responses. If you are studying AS Psychology the examinations are taken at the end of your 1-year course.

AS Paper 2

The AS topics approaches in psychology, biopsychology, psychopathology, research methods and data handling and analysis are assessed in a written 1½ hour exam in which 72 marks are awarded, comprising 50% of the AS. There are three sections in the exam, sections A, B, and C, comprising multiple-choice, short answer and extended writing questions.

A-level Paper 2

The topics approaches in psychology, biopsychology, research methods and data handling and analysis are assessed in a written 2-hour exam in which 96 marks are awarded comprising 33.3% of the A-level. There are three sections in the exam, sections A, B, and C, comprising multiple-choice, short answer and extended writing questions; 50% of the marks are awarded in section C which contains questions on research methods and data handling.

Assessment objectives: AO1, AO2 and AO3 skills

Assessment objectives (AOs) are set by Ofqual and are the same across all A-level Psychology specifications and all exam boards. The exams measure how you have achieved the assessment objectives outlined in the table below.

AO1	Demonstrate knowledge and understanding of scientific ideas, processes, techniques and procedures.
AO2	Apply knowledge and understanding of scientific ideas, processes, techniques and procedures in a theoretical context; in a practical context; when handling qualitative data and quantitative data.
AO3	Analyse, interpret and evaluate scientific information, ideas and evidence, including in relation to issues, to make judgements and reach conclusions and to develop and refine practical design and procedures

AO1 questions

Identify and **outline** two techniques that may be used in a cognitive interview.   (4 marks)

AO2 questions

Evaluate learning theory as an explanation of attachment.   (4 marks)

AO1 + AO2 questions

Describe and **evaluate** any two studies of social influence.   (12 marks)

AO1 + AO2 + AO3 questions

Outline and **evaluate** research into the effect of leading questions on the accuracy of eyewitness testimony.   (8 marks)

Multiple-choice questions

On both A-level and AS papers there are multiple-choice questions and you need to read these carefully. It is important not to jump to conclusions about an answer because one of the options may be a 'distractor'. For multiple-choice questions there will be four or five suggested answers, and usually you will be asked to shade in the 'box' applicable to the answer you suggest. For example:

Which **one** of the following statements is false?

A   The id is responsible for pleasure seeking behaviour.

B   The ego develops in the anal stage of development.

C   The superego causes us to behave badly.

D   The id causes selfish behaviour.

Examples of multiple-choice questions are included for each of the three topics. Answers are provided, with some commentary, on page 107.

Effective examination performance

Read the question carefully because marks are awarded only for the specific requirements of the question *as it is set*. Do not waste valuable time answering a question that you wish had been set.

Make a brief plan before you start writing an extended answer. There is space on the exam paper for planning. A plan can be as simple as a list of points, but you must know what, and how much, you plan to write. Time management in exams is vital.

Sometimes a question asks you to outline something. You should practise doing this in order to develop the skill of précis. Be aware of the difference between AO1, AO2 and AO3 commands (injunctions). You will lose marks if you treat AO2 commands such as **evaluate** as an opportunity to write more descriptive (AO1) content. Read the question command carefully and note the relevant skill requirement in your question plan (e.g. outline = AO1, describe = AO1, explain = AO2, evaluate = AO2/AO3).

Marks are awarded **in bands** for:

- AO1: the amount of relevant material presented. Low marks are awarded for brief or inappropriate material and high marks for accurate and detailed material.
- AO2: the level and effectiveness of critical commentary. Low marks are awarded for superficial consideration of a restricted range of issues and high marks for a good range of ideas and specialist terms, and effective use of material addressing a broad range of issues.
- AO3: the extent to which the answer demonstrates a thorough understanding of methods by which psychologists conduct research, for analysis, interpretation, explanation and evaluation of research methodologies and investigative activities.

Question 1 Approaches in psychology (1)

Multiple-choice questions

1.1 **Which of the following approaches best match the assumptions below? Choose one term that matches each statement.**   (5 marks)

If you are studying AS Psychology match options A–C only.

- **A** Biological approach
- **B** Behaviourist approach
- **C** Cognitive approach
- **D** Psychodynamic approach
- **E** Humanistic approach

Behaviour is motivated by conscious mental processes.

All behaviour is learned and can be unlearned.

Behaviour is motivated by forces in the unconscious mind.

Behaviour is motivated by the desire for self-actualisation and free will.

Behaviour can be explained by studying the functions of physiological systems.

1.2 Anton recently broke up with his girlfriend and has been very depressed. He avoids socialising and has been sleeping badly. He has exams soon but is pretty sure he will fail. After seeing his GP he has been referred to a psychologist.

Which one of the following therapies would be offered by a psychologist taking the cognitive approach? (1 mark)

A Psychoanalysis

B Systematic desensitisation

C Humanistic counselling

D CBT

E Drug treatment

1.3 Which one of the following terms is not associated with learning approaches? (1 mark)

A Reinforcement

B Classical conditioning

C Congruence

D Conditioned responses

E Stimulus-response learning

1.4 In the Watson and Raynor study, a loud noise was sounded while baby Albert played with a white rat and he learned to fear white rats.

In this study, which one of the following is the unconditioned stimulus? (1 mark)

A The loud noise

B The steel bar

C The white rat

D The fear response

Question 1.5 is not examined at AS.

1.5 Which one of the following terms is associated with humanistic approaches? (1 mark)

A Reinforcement

B Self-actualisation

C Learning

D Super-ego

E Schema

Question 2 Approaches in psychology (2)

Describe how learning approaches explain human behaviour. (6 marks)

ⓔ Question injunction = describe. This question requires you to show AO1 skills. You need to demonstrate your understanding of how learning approaches explain human behaviour. You are not expected to provide more than 5–6 minutes of writing.

Student A

The learning approach makes three assumptions. First, it assumes that all behaviour is learned; second, that what has been learned can be unlearned; and third, that abnormal behaviour is learned in the same way as normal behaviour. **a** Learning theorists take a behaviourist approach and behaviourists propose that behaviour is learned by classical conditioning, operant conditioning or social learning. **b** In classical conditioning, an unconditioned stimulus, such as an unexpected loud noise, triggers a natural reflex, such as the startle response and fear, but, if another stimulus, e.g. seeing a spider, occurs at the same time, this may in future elicit the fear response when a spider is seen. **c** In operant conditioning, behaviour is learned through the consequences of our actions, and in social learning behaviour is learned by observation. **d** Learning theorists believe that we are a product of our environment, that at birth we are a 'tabula rasa' or blank slate — our genetic make-up is largely ignored and our personality, IQ, achievements and behaviour are shaped by the environment in which we are reared. **e** Behaviourism is at the extreme end of nurture in the nature–nurture debate. **f**

e **6/6 marks awarded.** Student A leaves nothing to chance. The description is accurate, thorough and coherent. **a** The assumptions are accurately described. **b**, **c**, **d** The three ways that behaviour is learned are identified and accurately explained. **e**, **f** The student demonstrates knowledge and understanding of the assumptions of learning theory which are expanded and placed correctly on the nurture side of the nature–nurture debate.

Student B

The learning approach assumes that all behaviour is learned. **a** Behaviourists suggest that behaviour is learned by classical conditioning, operant conditioning or social learning. **b** Classical conditioning is stimulus–response learning, operant conditioning means that behaviour that causes pleasure is repeated and in social learning children learn by observing role models. **c** Learning theory says that all behaviour is caused by nurture not by nature. **d**

e **3/6 marks awarded.** **a**–**d** Student B has given an accurate but brief outline of the learning approach. This is not a top band answer because, although the answer is accurate, it lacks the detail required by the question injunction 'describe'.

Question 3 Approaches in psychology (3)

Evaluate learning approaches as an explanation of human behaviour. (6 marks)

e Question injunction = evaluate. This question requires you to show AO2 skills. You need to demonstrate your understanding of the strengths/weaknesses of learning approaches to explaining behaviour. For high marks you need to express your ideas clearly, using appropriate psychological terminology, to demonstrate a clear understanding. You can address either a broad range of issues in reasonable depth or a narrower range of issues in greater depth. You are not expected to write for more than 5–6 minutes.

Student A

A strength of learning approaches is that research evidence by Watson and Rayner demonstrates how phobic behaviour can be learned, supporting the assumption that behaviour can be learned. **a** Another advantage of the learning approach is that it is hopeful, as it suggests that abnormal behaviour can be unlearned and this approach has led to the development of practical applications, such as systematic desensitisation as a treatment for phobias. **b** However, learning approaches are deterministic because they ignore conscious reasoning, subjective experience and the idea that humans have the free will to choose how to behave and assume that we are 'programmed' to behave the way we do because of past experience. The approach is criticised as being dehumanising and mechanistic because people are reduced to programmed stimulus–response units. **c** Another disadvantage is that the learning approaches are reductionist because they ignore the role of innate and/or physiological individual differences (nature) and focus only on the role of environmental factors (nurture) as explanations for behaviour. **d**

e **5–6/6 marks awarded.** **a**–**d** The student has identified a range of issues and has commented on these issues in reasonable depth and in detail. There is a clear and coherent expression of ideas and the student uses a good range of psychological terms. One strength of the answer is that the student uses psychological terminology accurately to demonstrate a good understanding of learning approaches. **c**, **d** A further strength of the answer is that the student demonstrates, by clear and accurate explanation, a thorough understanding of why learning theories can be described as reductionist and deterministic. The answer could perhaps be improved by including an example of reductionist research such as Bandura's study of the social learning of aggressive behaviour or by making a comparison of learning approaches with another approach.

Student B

A strength of the learning approach is that it is hopeful, as it suggests that abnormal behaviour can be unlearned and this approach has led to the development of practical treatments for phobias. **a** However, learning approaches are deterministic because they assume we have no control over our behaviour or free will to choose behaviour. **b** Also learning approaches have low ecological validity because research, such as by Watson and Rayner, is done using lab experiments not in real life. **c** Another disadvantage is that learning approaches are reductionist because they ignore the role of biological and cognitive factors and suggest that all behaviour is caused by nurture not nature. **d**

e 3–4/6 marks awarded. **a** The student makes an accurate point but this point could have been expanded and/or supported by evidence. **b** The student identifies an appropriate issue but does not go on to explain or argue the point. **c** This point is inaccurate as it applies to *research studies* rather than to psychological approaches. This point demonstrates a lack of understanding of what is meant by ecological validity. **d** In the final sentence the student again makes an accurate point but does not expand, explain or argue the point thoroughly. Overall, the answer reads like a list of points rather than a coherent and well-explained evaluation.

Question 4 Approaches in psychology (4)

Discuss the contribution of cognitive psychologists to our understanding of human behaviour.

(16 marks)

e Question injunction = discuss. This question assesses AO2/AO3 skills, and marks are awarded for knowledge and understanding.

Your answer could include commentary on:

- how research by cognitive psychologists has increased understanding of human behaviour, using examples of research to support arguments
- how cognitive psychologists have developed treatments to help people recover from mental illness and the advantages of these treatments
- the advantages and limitations of the assumptions of the cognitive approach compared to one or more other approaches
- the methodological problems that arise when cognitive psychologists carry out research into mental processes
- research by cognitive psychologists in topics, such as memory and attachment, studied for Paper 1

For high marks you need to express your ideas clearly, using appropriate psychological terminology, to demonstrate a clear understanding. You can address either a broad range of issues in reasonable depth or a narrower range of issues in greater depth. Your answer must be evaluative rather than descriptive and you should allow a few minutes to write a plan before you begin writing your answer.

Student A

Cognitive psychologists study the human mind. They assume the mind is like an information processor and that people have free will to control how they think and behave. Cognitive psychologists adopt an information processing approach, studying sensory input, inferring some sort of mental process, and recording behavioural outputs in topics such as perception, attention, language and memory. **a** An example of how cognitive psychologists have contributed to our understanding is the Loftus and Palmer study of eyewitness memory, which demonstrated how, by asking witnesses leading questions, a false memory could be created, and how unreliable eyewitness testimony is. **b**

Cognitive psychologists have also increased our understanding of why we forget information and suggest that we forget, not because the memory has gone, but because information in long-term memory cannot be remembered because retrieval cues are not present. c Cognitive psychologists have shown that when we store a new memory we also store retrieval cues about the environmental context and our physical state, and that information is more likely to be retrieved from long-term memory if, when we try to remember, the appropriate retrieval cues are present. d This led to the development of the cognitive interview by which witnesses to events such as crimes are helped to recall many more details than would be the case in a standard police interview. e

Another way that cognitive psychologists have increased our understanding is by explaining how mental schemas influence our behaviour. e Schemas are mental representations that allow us to organise thoughts, categorise events and predict outcomes. Our schemas start in early life and we add to them continually throughout life, developing new ones and adapting existing ones. f In attachment theory, Bowlby believed that an attachment creates an internal working model (a cognitive schema) for all future relationships and that this first attachment forms a template or schema that gives the child a feel for what all future relationships will be like. This theory is useful as it emphasises the importance of early child relationships. g Schema theory is also useful as it can explain individual differences, because schemas are not always accurate representations, but are individual interpretations which are prone to distortion. h

In sum, cognitive psychologists have found many useful applications, ranging from advice about the validity of eyewitness testimony to how to improve memory. One of their most useful contributions is cognitive behavioural therapies for psychological problems such as depression and anxiety. j

An advantage of cognitive psychology is that it takes a scientific approach, and usually uses laboratory experiments to reveal mental processes, for example, participants will take part in memory tests in strictly controlled conditions. k This means that cognitive research is especially useful because it tends to be reliable. l For example, Loftus and Palmer carried out their research using high levels of control and standardised procedures, leading to research that could be repeated to verify the findings. m However, it is important to remember that mental processes cannot be observed, they can only be inferred and biological psychologists would argue that to understand human behaviour we should study the physical brain rather than the metaphysical mind. n

Another criticism of cognitive psychology is that we cannot assume that rational thought processes are the cause of all behaviour. Biological psychologists have shown that the structure and function of biological sensory systems also influence behaviour. o Also, unlike cognitive psychologists, psychodynamic psychologists, such as Freud, assume that unconscious processes, such as ego defence mechanisms, or conflict between the id, ego and superego, motivate human behaviour, which suggests that people are unaware of, and cannot always describe, their mental processes. p

ⓔ 14–16/16 marks awarded. Student A has written a wide-ranging discussion clearly focused on the question. **ⓐ–ⓑ** In the first paragraph, the assumptions of cognitive psychologists are outlined and an accurate example is given to show how research has increased our understanding. **ⓒ–ⓔ** In the second paragraph, the student explains in accurate detail how cognitive psychologists have increased our understanding of forgetting and has given an appropriate example of how the research has been applied. **ⓔ–ⓗ** The third paragraph is a synoptic paragraph linking cognitive schema to developmental psychology, demonstrating breadth of knowledge and understanding. **ⓙ** Here the answer summarises the ways in which cognitive psychologists have increased understanding. **ⓚ–ⓝ** In the next paragraph, the student evaluates research by cognitive psychologists, linking this to its usefulness, and makes an accurate counter argument about the issues related to researching mental processes. The final paragraph is perhaps the weakest. **ⓞ** The student could have expanded by giving an example of behaviour that biological rather than cognitive psychologists can explain. **ⓟ** The final sentence accurately suggesting that not all mental processes are conscious is a well-explained counter argument, but a final sentence referring back to the question would have given a stronger end to the answer. However, overall this is a thorough, effective, coherent and well written answer.

Student B

Cognitive psychologists study the human mind and memory. **ⓐ** An example of how cognitive psychologists have contributed to our understanding is the Loftus and Palmer study of eyewitness memory, which showed that asking leading questions can cause false memories. **ⓑ** Cognitive psychologists can also explain why we forget **ⓒ** because when we store a new memory we also store retrieval cues and information is more likely to be retrieved from memory if, when we try to remember, the appropriate retrieval cues are present. **ⓓ**

Another way that cognitive psychologists have increased our understanding is by explaining how mental schemas influence our behaviour. **ⓔ** In attachment theory, Bowlby believed that an attachment creates an internal working model (a cognitive schema) for all future relationships and that this first attachment forms a template or schema that gives the child a feel for what all future relationships will be like. This theory is useful as it emphasises the importance of early child relationships. **ⓕ**

An advantage of cognitive psychology is it uses laboratory experiments to reveal mental processes, for example, participants will take part in memory tests in strictly controlled conditions. **ⓖ** This means that cognitive research is especially useful because it tends to be reliable. **ⓗ**

However, not all psychologists agree with the cognitive approach. Biological psychologists argue that to understand human behaviour we should study the physical brain rather than the metaphysical mind **ⓙ** and have shown that the structure and function of biological sensory systems also influence behaviour. **ⓚ** Psychodynamic psychologists, such as Freud, assume that unconscious processes, such as ego defence mechanisms, or conflict between the id, ego and superego motivate human behaviour, and social psychologists assume that other people influence our behaviour. **ⓛ**

ⓔ **9/16 marks awarded.** ⓐ–ⓗ In the first three paragraphs, Student B has written quite an effective answer, focusing on the contribution of cognitive psychology and supporting the points made with evidence and some argument. ⓘ–ⓙ The weak point of the answer is in the fourth paragraph, which, although it accurately argues that other approaches do not agree with cognitive psychologists, is not focused clearly on the stem of the question 'the contribution of cognitive psychologists to increasing understanding'. A final sentence such as 'although cognitive psychologists have made useful contributions to understanding a wide range of behaviours, they cannot offer a full explanation of all behaviours' would strengthen this answer.

Question 5 Biopsychology (1)

Multiple-choice questions

5.1 A neuron is a specialised nerve cell that receives, processes and transmits information to other cells in the body. Which **three** of the following statements are true of sensory neurons?   (3 marks)

    A   Carry messages in only one direction

    B   Are afferent neurons

    C   Carry messages both to and from the brain

    D   Send information to motor neurons

    E   Receive information through dendrites of other neurons

5.2 Neurotransmitters are biochemical substances that have an effect on mental health. Match the following neurotransmitters to the correct outline of their function.   (4 marks)

    A   Dopamine

    B   Epinephrine

    C   Serotonin

    D   Endorphins

    Involved in mood, sleep and appetite and depression and anxiety disorders

    Involved in pain relief and feelings of pleasure and contentedness

    Correlated with movement, attention and learning

    Involved in energy and glucose metabolism

5.3 The fight or flight response is a chain of rapidly occurring physiological reactions that mobilise the body's resources to deal with threatening circumstances. In which part of the nervous system does the fight or flight response originate?   (1 mark)

    A   The endocrine system

    B   The sympathetic nervous system

    C   The pancreas

    D   The brain

Questions 5.4 and 5.5 are not examined at AS.

5.4 The human brain is divided into four lobes. Which one of the following is not one of these? (1 mark)

A   The frontal   D   The occipital

B   The brainstem   E   The parietal

C   The temporal

5.5 Biological rhythms are maintained by endogenous pacemakers and exogenous zeitgebers. Which **four** of the following are examples of exogenous zeitgebers? (4 marks)

A   The seasons of the year   D   Social norms

B   The amount of daylight   E   Alarm clock

C   Hormones

Question 6 Biopsychology (2)

Outline the structures and processes involved in neurotransmission. (6 marks)

ⓔ Question injunction = outline. This question requires you to show AO1 skills. You need to demonstrate your knowledge of how information is sent between the brain and the body and between nerve cells. You are not expected to provide more than 5–6 minutes of writing. You could include information on:

- the synaptic cleft
- pre- and postsynaptic membranes; postsynaptic receptor sites
- neurotransmitters and release of neurotransmitters
- action potentials
- sensory neurons
- motor neurons

Student A

Neurotransmission is how information is sent between nerve cells (neurons) in the brain and body. ⓐ Neurons are only capable of carrying a message in one direction. ⓑ Sensory neurons relay information to the brain and motor neurons carry information from the brain to the body. Interneurons relay information from sensory neurons to motor neurons. ⓒ In pre-synaptic processes, information comes to the neuron through the dendrites from other neurons and on to the cell body (soma) which processes information and then passes it along the axon. ⓓ At the end of the axon are structures called terminal buttons that pass the information on to glands, muscles, or other neurons. Information between neurons is carried by biochemical substances called neurotransmitters such as dopamine and serotonin. ⓔ In the post-synaptic process, when the neurotransmitter leaves the axon it passes through the synapse and then on to the dendrite receptor sites where it may, or may not, activate the receptor neuron. ⓕ

ⓔ **5–6/6 marks awarded.** Student A has written an accurate and thorough answer. ⓐ–ⓕ Knowledge of both the structures and processes involved in synaptic transmission, including reference to both pre-synaptic and post-synaptic processes, is generally accurate and mostly well detailed. The answer is clear and coherent. Specialist terminology is used effectively. **i** The answer could have been improved here had the student expanded on the rather vague last point 'may or may not' activate the receptor neuron by including information on action potentials.

Student B

Some neurons relay information to the brain and some neurons carry information from the brain to the body. **a** Information comes to the neuron through the dendrites and then passes along the axon of the receiving neuron. **b** Information between neurons is carried by neurotransmitters which are biochemical substances. **c**

---

e **2/6 marks awarded.** Student B has written a very brief answer. **a–c** The points made here though accurate are vague. The lack of detail in the answer suggests that the student's knowledge of structures and/or processes involved in synaptic transmission is limited.

Question 7 Biopsychology (3)

Penny was wandering down a village lane towards the local shop. Suddenly, out of nowhere, a huge black dog ran towards her snarling and barking. Terrified, Penny ran away as fast as she could. She wasn't very fit and she was amazed how fast she ran. A friend later told her that it was *the fight or flight response* that helped her escape.

Describe how the fight or flight response helped Penny run so fast.   (6 marks)

e Question injunction = describe. This question requires you to show AO1 skills. You need to demonstrate your knowledge of the physiological reactions that comprise the fight or flight response. You are not expected to provide more than 5–6 minutes of writing.

Student A

The fight or flight response is a chain of rapidly occurring physiological reactions, originating in the hypothalamus, that mobilise the body's resources to deal with a threat. **a** In response to threat, the body's sympathetic nervous system is activated due to the sudden release of hormones .**b** The sympathetic branch of the nervous system stimulates the adrenal gland to release adrenaline, noradrenaline and corticosteroids into the bloodstream. **c** The increase in adrenaline produces the physiological reactions, such as increased heart rate, breathing and blood pressure and a dry mouth, known as the 'fight or flight' response. **d** The increase in heart rate results in more blood to the muscles which helped Penny run faster than she would normally. **e**

---

e **5–6/6 marks awarded.** Student A has written an accurate and thorough answer. **a**, **b** The student correctly identifies the hypothalamus as the source of the fight or flight response and states that the sympathetic nervous system is activated. **c**, **d** The student accurately describes the hormones produced and the function of adrenaline. **e** The student demonstrates knowledge and understanding by correctly describing how adrenaline helped Penny run faster.

Student B

The fight or flight response happens when we are threatened. Heart rate increases, breathing becomes faster and pupils dilate for better vision. **a** Adrenaline and corticosteroids are released into the bloodstream and in an instant, your body is prepared to either fight or flee. **b**

e **2–3/6 marks awarded.** Student B has written a very brief answer and has not really answered the question because the physiological response is not explicitly linked to Penny's ability to run faster. **a**, **b** These are accurate statements that read like a list.

Question 8 Biopsychology (4)

This is not examined at AS.

Outline how split-brain studies investigated the effect of disconnecting the two hemispheres of the brain.

(4 marks)

e Question injunction = outline. This question requires you to show AO1 skills. You need to demonstrate your knowledge of how the procedures in Sperry were used. You are not expected to provide more than about 4 minutes of writing. You should include:

- the procedure and equipment used
- the controls used
- the tasks
- the behaviours recorded

Student A

The left hemisphere controls the right side of the body and the right visual field. The right hemisphere controls the left side of the body and the left visual field. Sperry used split-brain patients to find out what happens when the two hemispheres are disconnected. The split-brain procedure is a surgical procedure called a commisurotomy to cut the corpus callosum which connects the two hemispheres. The participants were people who suffered from severe epilepsy who had a commisurotomy. **a** Participants were tested individually. Pictures were presented to the left or right of a screen thus to the left or right visual field. **b** The participant covered one eye and looked at a fixed point in the centre of a projection screen. Images were projected to the right or the left of the screen at a high speed. **c** Below the screen there was a gap so that the participant could touch and feel objects but not see his or her hands. **d** Each time an image was presented the participant was asked — had they seen the image before, to describe what they could see, to identify a matching object with their left or right hand. **e** Sperry recorded and analysed the behaviours to see whether the functions of the left and right hemispheres could be identified. **f**

ⓔ **4/4 marks awarded.** Student A has written an accurate and very thorough answer. **a** The student accurately describes the split-brain operation. **b**, **c**, **d** The student describes the procedure clearly and concisely. **e**, **f** The student outlines the tasks given to the participants and demonstrates knowledge and understanding of how Sperry used the data to identify the functions of the left and right hemispheres.

Student B

Sperry used split-brain patients who were people with severe epilepsy who had a commisurotomy. **a** The participants sat in front of the screen, covered one eye and images were projected to the right or the left of the screen. **b** Each time an image was presented the participant was asked to describe what they could see. **c**

ⓔ 2/4 marks awarded. **a–c** Student B has written an accurate but very brief answer that does not make it clear how this procedure can be used to investigate split-brain behaviour. There is no mention of visual fields or of the difference between the left and right hemisphere. The answer is too brief.

Question 9 Biopsychology (5)

This is not examined at AS.

Outline two ways of studying the brain. (4 marks)

ⓔ Question injunction = outline. This question requires you to show AO1 skills. You need to demonstrate your knowledge of two ways by which the brain can be studied. You are not expected to provide more than about 4 minutes of writing. You could include:

- post-mortem studies
- electroencephalogram (EEG)
- functional magnetic resonance imaging (fMRI)

Student A

One way to study the brain is to carry out a post-mortem study of the brain after someone has died. Researchers look at parts of the brain they believe may have been involved in illness, or may have been damaged by the environment. Post-mortem studies of the brain allow researchers to look at the brain in ways which are not possible in a living patient. Post-mortem studies require the consent of the individual before their death or from their family. **a**

Another way to study the brain is by electroencephalography (EEG). An EEG records the electrical activity along the scalp and current flows within the neurons of the brain. EEG is often used to diagnose sleep disorders and brain death. During EEG brain responses to stimuli can be measured by looking at event-related potential (ERP) which is the measured brain reaction to some sort of stimulus. **b**

ⓔ **4/4 marks awarded.** Student A has written an accurate and thorough answer. **a** The student gives a clear, accurate and concise outline of post-mortem studies. **b** The student also gives a clear, accurate and concise outline of how EEG is used to study the brain.

An alternative answer could have described functional magnetic resonance imaging (fMRI).

Student B

One way to study the brain is to carry out a post-mortem study of the brain after someone has died. Post-mortem studies of the brain allow researchers to look at the brain in ways which are not possible in a living patient. Post-mortem studies require the consent of the individual before their death or from their family. a

Another way to study the brain is by MRI scan. MRI scans produce pictures of the brain which researchers can study. b

e **1–2/4 marks awarded.** Student B's answer is very brief. a Here, the answer is accurate but gives no detail of how a post-mortem study may be used. b The student only identifies a method of studying the brain and this point is not worthy of credit. The answer could have been written by someone who has not studied psychology.

Question 10 Research methods, scientific processes, data handling and inferential statistics (1)

The curious teacher

A psychology teacher wondered whether the way desks are arranged in a classroom influences how much students learn. She set out the desks in one classroom in rows and in another classroom in a circle. Over 3 weeks she taught the same memory topics to two classes and then set all the students the same test. There were 20 students in each class and the test was marked out of 50.

10.1 Which one of the following research methods did the teacher use? (1 mark)

    A Case study   **D** Field experiment

    B Correlation   **E** Observation

    C Laboratory experiment

10.2 Which one of the following statements identifies the experimental design used by the curious teacher? (1 mark)

    A Repeated measures design

    B Matched participant design

    C Independent design

    D Experimental design

10.3 In the research by the curious teacher, which one of the following statements identifies the independent variable? (1 mark)

    A The marks out of 50 on the test

    B The memory topics

    C Whether the desks are in rows or a circle

    D Whether a student was absent

Questions & Answers

Question 10.4 is not examined at AS.

10.4 In the research by the curious teacher, which **three** of the following statements describe the type of data collected? (3 marks)

A   Nominal level data
B   Quantitative data
C   Ordinal level data

D   Qualitative data
E   Numerical data

10.5 The psychology teacher was surprised because the results of the test showed little difference between the two classes. She decided to continue her research and she asked a trainee teacher to sit at the back of each class for two lessons on memory to observe students' behaviour. The trainee teacher recorded on a tally chart each time a student (a) asked a question, (b) answered a question, (c) talked to another student.

Which **two** of the following statements identify the type of observation carried out by the trainee teacher? (2 marks)

A   Naturalistic observation
B   Overt observation
C   Covert observation

D   Participant observation
E   Non-participant observation

10.6 Which one of the following statements identifies the sampling technique used by the curious teacher? (1 mark)

A   Random sample
B   Quota sample
C   Volunteer sample

D   Opportunity sample
E   Matched sample

10.7 The curious teacher set the students another test on memory and when the test was completed she compared the two sets of test scores. Which **two** of the following statements identify measures of central tendency? (2 marks)

A   Standard deviation
B   The mean scores
C   The range
D   The median scores
E   The total marks for each class

Question 10.8 is not examined at AS.

10.8 Which one of the following inferential tests could the curious teacher use to find out whether any difference between the scores of the two classes is significant? (1 mark)

A   Spearman's rho
B   Related t-test
C   Mann-Whitney U test
D   Chi Squared
E   Sign test

Question 11 Research methods, scientific processes, data handling and inferential statistics (2)

Psychological research suggests that information in short-term memory (STM) is acoustically encoded (by sound). In an attempt to test this, 10 participants were asked to read and then recall two lists of 10 words — List A and List B.

The 10 words in List A were: beat, feet, greet, heat, leap, meet, neat, peat, seat, wheat

The 10 words in List B were: barn, cell, diet, fish, jump, lamb, mast, poll, riot, show

All the participants first read and then recalled the words in List A, then after a short break they read and then recalled the words in List B.

A table of results is given below.

Participant	Number of words recalled in List A	Number of words recalled in List B
1	4	7
2	3	5
3	5	5
4	3	6
5	2	7
6	5	7
7	7	6
8	5	6
9	4	8
10	3	5

11.1 Look at the words in each of the lists and explain why the researcher selected those words. (3 marks)

e Question injunction = explain. This question assesses AO2 and AO3 skills. One AO2 mark is awarded for your analysis of unfamiliar material in recognising the basis for the selection of words. Two AO3 marks are awarded if you demonstrate your understanding of how and why the IV has been operationalised.

> **Student A**
>
> The researcher selected the words so that the words in List A are all acoustically similar but the words in List B are not acoustically similar. **a** These words were selected because if information in STM is encoded acoustically, the words from List A would be confused and fewer words would be remembered, but the words in List B would not be confused and would be remembered better. **b**

e **3/3 marks awarded: 1 (AO2) mark + 2 (AO3) marks. a, b** Student A has correctly identified the difference between the words in List A and List B and has then explained why this difference was selected. This answer demonstrates knowledge and understanding of what is being investigated (acoustic encoding in STM) and how this (the DV) was operationalised.

Student B

The researcher selected the words because all the words in List A sound similar but the words in List B do not sound similar. a

ⓔ **1/3 marks awarded.** a Student B has correctly identified the difference between the words in List A and List B but has not explained why this difference was selected.

11.2 Explain how you would use descriptive statistics to summarise the findings of this investigation. (4 marks)

ⓔ Question injunction = explain. This question assesses AO3 skills and you should show, in detail, your understanding of how data can be summarised. Marks are awarded for demonstrating knowledge of descriptive statistics and how they are used to analyse data. You could suggest and explain the use of appropriate measures of central tendency and/or appropriate measures of dispersion.

Student A

Researchers could calculate measures of central tendency by calculating and comparing the mean of the words remembered in List A and List B conditions to show whether there is a difference in the average number of words remembered in the similar and not similar conditions. a

Also, because the data are ordinal level, the researcher could compare the range of words remembered in List A and in List B to show whether there is a difference in measures of dispersion. If there is a difference in ranges this might suggest individual differences in the memory of participants. b

ⓔ **4/4 marks awarded.** Student A's answer is accurate and detailed. a The answer correctly suggests a measure of central tendency (the mean) and explains how this can be used in the context of the study. b The student has suggested that the range be calculated — and has justified this by explaining what the range will show. The answer demonstrates knowledge and understanding and is clear and coherent.

Student B

Researchers could calculate and compare the mean and the range of the words remembered in List A and List B conditions, a and draw a scattergram to show the findings. b

ⓔ **1/4 marks awarded.** Student B's answer is very brief. a Although the student has suggested a measure of central tendency (the mean), this is not explained. Also, the student has suggested that the range be calculated — but has not explained why. b The comment about 'draw a scattergram' demonstrates a lack of understanding of methodology and data analysis, as the investigation is not a correlational design.

11.3 **The table below shows the findings of the study.**

	Number of words recalled in List A — similar	Number of words recalled in List B — not similar
Mean	4.1	6.2
Range	5	3

What conclusions might the psychologist draw from these findings? Explain what the data appear to show. (4 marks)

ⓔ Question injunction = explain. This question assesses AO3 skills and you must demonstrate that you can interpret the data to explain what the findings of this investigation may mean. Marks are awarded for identification of a difference in performance between the conditions (measures of central tendency in List A and List B) and for explaining why this may have occurred and what it may mean. Marks are also awarded if you identify any differences in the dispersion of the two sets of scores (ranges) and then explain what this may imply.

Student A

The mean number of the List A (acoustically similar) words remembered was 4.1 but the mean number of List B (acoustically dissimilar) words was 6.2. **ⓐ** This suggests that the acoustic similarity made the words harder to remember than the acoustically dissimilar words and supports the idea that information in STM is coded acoustically. **ⓑ** However, the range of scores in List A was greater than in List B (List A is 5 while List B is 3). **ⓒ** This suggests variation in whether the acoustic similarity of words affects how well they are remembered because the same participants took part in both conditions, which excludes participant differences. **ⓓ**

ⓔ **4/4 marks awarded.** Student A has given a clear and detailed answer, demonstrating breadth of understanding of the data and what they may mean. **ⓐ**, **ⓑ** The explanation of the difference in the mean scores is coherent and is accurately elaborated in terms of the aim of the research. **ⓒ**, **ⓓ** The explanation of the difference in the range of scores is a strength of the answer because the student demonstrates understanding of both the repeated measures design and the research aim.

Student B

Only four of the ten participants remembered five or more words in List A, but all ten participants remembered five or more words in List B. **ⓐ** This suggests that List B words were easier to remember than List A words — possibly because they didn't sound the same. **ⓑ**

ⓔ **1–2/4 marks awarded.** **ⓐ**, **ⓑ** Student B has provided a very brief answer, but has done 'some work' and demonstrates some understanding of the data. The answer gives a basic explanation — 'because they [the words in List B] didn't sound the same' — but this explanation could have been much more clearly expressed.

Questions & Answers

11.4 **Identify the research design used in this study.** (1 mark)

ℯ Question injunction = 'identify'. This question assesses AO1 skills and whether you know the difference between different types of investigation design.

> **Student A**
>
> The investigation of memory was a repeated measures design as the same participants took part in both conditions.

ℯ **1/1 mark awarded.** Student A has given the correct answer, but wasted time giving an explanation which was not asked for.

> **Student B**
>
> Matched participant design because the same participants took part in both conditions.

ℯ **0/1 marks awarded.** Student B gives the wrong answer and demonstrates a common error. Students frequently confuse repeated measures designs with matched participant designs. The student also wastes time by giving an explanation which is, in any case, incorrect. The answer would be awarded no marks.

11.5 **Explain one disadvantage of using this experimental design in the study and explain how the researcher could have overcome this disadvantage.** (6 marks)

ℯ Question injunction = explain. This question assesses AO3 skills and whether you understand the kinds of problem that psychologists have to overcome when designing research. Your knowledge of the advantages and limitations of independent and repeated measures design could be used to answer this question: 3 marks are awarded for an appropriate disadvantage and 3 marks for explaining how this disadvantage could be overcome.

> **Student A**
>
> One weakness of the repeated measures design, in which all the participants first remembered List A, the similar words, and then remembered List B, the not-similar words, **a** is that this design could lead to 'order effects' because participants might improve with practice, which could explain why participants performed better on List B. **b** This weakness could be overcome by having half of the participants remember List A followed by List B and half of the participants remembering List B followed by List A. **c**

ℯ **5/6 marks awarded.** Student A's answer is clear and detailed, demonstrating an understanding of one weakness of repeated measures design. **a**–**c** The strength of the answer is that the student identifies the weakness, explains why this is a weakness and then gives an appropriate suggestion for how the weakness may be overcome. Although the student does not use the term 'counterbalancing', and does not explain how counterbalancing controls for order effects, the answer demonstrates understanding.

Student B

One disadvantage of the investigation is there were only ten participants, which is a very small sample, so the results cannot be generalised. To overcome this, a larger sample should be used in an independent design.

e **0/6 marks awarded.** Student B has not read the question carefully and has not answered the question set. The question asks for a disadvantage of the design of the investigation, which requires the answer to refer to the repeated measures design. Although the answer briefly refers to using an independent design the answer demonstrates a lack of understanding.

11.6 Discuss the value of laboratory experiments in cognitive psychology. (6 marks)

e Question injunction = discuss. This question assesses both AO3 and AO2 skills. The key phrases in the question are:

■ discuss
■ the value of laboratory experiments

You need to demonstrate your knowledge and understanding of research methods (how science works). You could:

■ identify/describe features of the experimental method
■ describe how the IV is isolated and manipulated
■ describe ways by which the DV is operationalised/measured
■ refer to the advantages and disadvantages of collecting quantitative data
■ refer to the control of extra variables
■ refer to the realism of the procedures
■ use your knowledge of other laboratory experiments in cognitive psychology, such as studies of memory and of eyewitness testimony (EWT), to show how private mental processes can be revealed in controlled laboratory experiments

To gain AO2/AO3 marks you need to evaluate the use of laboratory experiments in cognitive psychology. You could refer to:

■ the strengths and limitations of laboratory-based experiments
■ the usefulness of laboratory-based experiments in increasing understanding of aspects of cognitive psychology (e.g. memory, EWT, improving memory)
■ evidence from naturalistic studies that either supports or contradicts the findings of laboratory experiments

Student A

During a laboratory experiment, researchers try to control all the variables except the independent variable (IV), which is the difference between the experimental conditions. Then the experimenter measures the effect of the IV on the DV, which is what is measured. One advantage of laboratory experiments is that researchers can control extraneous variables that might affect the IV or the DV, thus they can be sure that any effect on the DV is caused by the IV and not by some uncontrolled variable. This is an advantage because statements about cause and effect can be made. **a** In addition, in laboratory experiments control groups can be established, as for example, in the Loftus and Palmer second experiment, where the use of a control group allowed the researchers to be sure that it was the use of the word 'smashed' that caused more participants to report seeing broken glass that wasn't present on the film. **b** This research was valuable because it demonstrated that the way eyewitnesses are questioned can affect the accuracy of their recall. Moreover, controlled laboratory experiments can be repeated to check that the findings are reliable (have not just happened by chance). **c**

However, laboratory experiments have low external validity because the procedures used may not measure how people behave outside the laboratory in their everyday lives. **d** For example, in the research into how information is encoded in memory (Baddeley), participants were asked to remember lists of words, but people don't often have to remember lists of words in their everyday lives. **e** That said, it is difficult to see how cognitive psychologists could investigate the encoding of information in memory by naturalistic methods such as by observational studies, and laboratory investigations of encoding, capacity and duration of information in memory have increased our knowledge about human memory. **f**

e **5–6/6 marks awarded.** Student A has given a highly effective answer. **a**, **b** The student provides a description of the main characteristics of laboratory experiments and, to demonstrate understanding, quotes Loftus and Palmer as an accurate example of research in which a control group was established, and why this control group was useful. **c** The student then explains how the Loftus and Palmer research was useful, which addresses the question of the value of laboratory experiments. **d**–**f** The student continues to identify and discuss a range of issues focusing on the strengths and weaknesses of laboratory experiments, and each issue is explained in reasonable depth. **e** The introduction of Baddeley in the discussion of external validity is an effective use of material (informed commentary), demonstrating knowledge and understanding. **f** The final sentence, arguing that human memory cannot be observed, demonstrates knowledge of research methods and again focuses on the question of the value of laboratory experiments. The strength of this answer is the clarity and coherence of the discussion.

Student B

In a laboratory experiment, researchers try to control all the variables except the independent variable (IV), which is the difference between the experimental conditions. Then the experimenter measures the effect of the IV on the DV, which is what is measured. One advantage of laboratory experiments is that researchers can control other variables that might affect the IV or the DV, thus they can be sure that any effect on the DV is caused by the IV and not by some uncontrolled variable. **a** Also, laboratory experiments can be repeated to check that the findings are reliable. **b**

However, laboratory experiments have low external validity because the procedures used may not measure how people behave outside the laboratory in their everyday lives. **c** For example, when researching memory, participants are often asked to remember lists of words, but people don't often have to remember lists of words in their everyday lives. Also, participants in laboratory experiments know their behaviour is being studied and this can give rise to demand characteristics because participants look for clues in the experiment to tell them how they are expected to behave. **d**

e **3–4/6 marks awarded.** **a**–**d** Student B provides a fairly effective discussion, comprising a brief outline of the main characteristics of laboratory experiments and a reasonably effective evaluation of the methodology. A range of issues, focusing on the strengths and weaknesses of laboratory experiments, is discussed, some in limited depth. Psychological terminology is used accurately and the student demonstrates knowledge and some understanding of research methods. The weakness of the answer is that the student does not address the question of the value of laboratory experiments to cognitive psychologists in an explicit manner, and the answer would be strengthened had the student quoted research evidence to support his or her arguments.

11.7 Write a suitable hypothesis for this study. (3 marks)

e The hypothesis must be testable and operationalised.

Student A

That when participants are given two lists of ten words to remember, there is NO difference in the number of similar sounding words remembered compared to the number of not-similar sounding words remembered.

e **3/3 marks awarded.** Student A has written a fully operationalised null hypothesis which is suitable. The student would also be awarded 3 marks had the alternative hypothesis been written.

Student B

That participants will remember less similar words than not-similar words.

ⓔ **2/3 marks awarded.** Student B has written a one-tailed alternative hypothesis that is appropriate but is not fully operationalised.

Question 12 Research methods, scientific processes, data handling and inferential statistics (3)

A sport psychologist wanted to find out whether physical exercise affects mood. To test this he put up a poster in a local sports club. The poster asked for people aged between 18 and 30 who are interested in the benefits of sport to contact him by e-mail on <u>sportypsychologist@youknowwhere.com</u>. When people contacted him he set up individual meetings in the sports club with each of the first 20 respondents. When they met he asked them to complete a questionnaire comprising 7 questions. The critical question was:

Please circle the number that best fits your mood at the moment.

| 1 | 2 | 3 | 4 | 5 | 6 | 7 | 8 | 9 | 10 |

Anxious   Relaxed

After completing the questionnaire each participant was asked to run 100 metres on a running track as fast as they comfortably could. After the run the participants were asked to complete a second questionnaire which, with other questions, also contained the same question about mood.

When 20 participants had taken part the psychologist analysed the results which were as follows:

	Mood before exercise	Mood after exercise
Mean score	4.2	7.1
Range	3	6

12.1 Identify the independent variable and the dependent variable in this study.   (2 marks)

ⓔ 1 mark for correct identification of each variable.

> **Student A**
>
> The independent variable is whether the mood of the participant is measured before or after they ran 100 metres.
>
> The dependent variable is the self-rated mood score of 1–10, where 1 = anxious and 10 = relaxed, of the participants before and after they ran 100 metres.

ⓔ **2/2 marks awarded.** Student A's answer is clear and accurate.

> **Student B**
>
> The independent variable is running 100 metres. The dependent variable is the mood of the participant before and after they ran.

ℯ 1/2 marks awarded. The independent variable is incorrect. The dependent variable is correct but could have been described more fully.

12.2 Write a suitable null hypothesis for this study.   (3 marks)

ℯ The null hypothesis must be testable and operationalised.

Student A
There is no significant difference in the reported mood scores of participants, on a 1–10 scale, where 1 = anxious and 10 = relaxed, before and after they run 100 metres.

ℯ 3/3 marks awarded. This is a testable null hypothesis in which the operationalised IV and DV are both accurate and clear.

Student B
There is no difference in the mood scores of participants before and after exercise.

ℯ 1/3 marks awarded. This is a null hypothesis but it is not testable because the operationalised IV and DV are not included.

12.3 Identify the sampling technique used in this study and explain one disadvantage of using this sampling technique.   (4 marks)

ℯ Question injunction = identify and explain. This assesses AO1 and AO3 skills.

AO1 = 1 mark for correct identification of the sampling technique. AO3 = 3 marks for explaining one disadvantage of the technique. This question assesses whether you understand the sampling techniques used by psychologists and the advantages and limitations of different sampling techniques.

Student A
The sampling technique used by the sports psychologist was a self-selecting sample (volunteer sample) because participants put themselves forward having seen the poster in the sports club. One disadvantage of using a self-selecting sample is that the sample will be biased. In this study it is probable that because the poster was put up in a sports club, all the participants will be sports enthusiasts who believe sport is beneficial to health **a** and it is unlikely that people who do not like or enjoy sport will even see the poster. **b** Having a biased sample is a disadvantage as being unrepresentative of the larger population the results are less generalisable and the psychologist will not be able to suggest that exercise will improve the mood of everyone. **c**

ℯ 3/4 marks awarded. Student A's answer is clear and detailed, demonstrating an understanding of one disadvantage of self-selected samples. **a–c** The strength of the answer is that the student correctly identifies the sampling technique, and then explains the effect of the disadvantage using psychological terms accurately.

Questions & Answers

> **Student B**
>
> The sample was random sample because the participants were just people who read the poster. **a** One disadvantage of using a random sample is that we can't control individual differences. **b**

e **0/4 marks awarded.** Student B has given the wrong answer because this is not a random sample. Even though the disadvantage is brief and accurate no marks can be awarded.

Question 12.4 is not examined at AS.

12.4 Name an appropriate statistical test that could be used to analyse the significance of the findings. Explain why the test you chose would be a suitable test for this research. (4 marks)

e Question injunction = identify and explain. This assesses AO1 and AO3 skills.

AO1 = 1 mark for correct identification of a statistical test. AO3 = 3 marks for explaining, in the context of the study, why this is a suitable choice of test.

> **Student A**
>
> An appropriate statistical test would be a Wilcoxon t-test. **a** This non-parametric test is appropriate because the research design was repeated measures, two mood scores were obtained from each participant, and also because the small sample cannot assume that scores are normally distributed. **b** The Wilcoxon t-test will allow the researcher to calculate the significance of the difference between the two ordinal level data sets of scores. **c**

e **4/4 marks awarded.** Student A's answer is correct. **a** The student correctly identifies an appropriate statistical test. **b**, **c** The student gives an accurate and detailed explanation for why the test is appropriate.

> **Student B**
>
> An appropriate statistical test would be a Mann–Whitney U test. **a** This test is appropriate because the test will allow the researcher to calculate the significance of the difference between the two sets of scores. **b**

e **0/4 marks awarded.** Student B's answer is incorrect. **a** The student selects a test that is appropriate only for an independent design. **b** The student gives a brief explanation which, had the suggested test been correct, might have been awarded 1 mark.

Question 12.5 is not examined at AS.

12.5 The difference in the mood scores before and after exercise were found to be significant at p=< 0.05. Explain what is meant by significant at p=< 0.05. (2 marks)

e Question injunction = explain. This assesses AO3 skills. Two marks are awarded for an accurate explanation.

Student A

There is a less than or equal to 5% probability that the difference in the mood scores occurred by chance rather than as a result of the exercise.

@ **2/2 marks awarded.** Student A's answer is correct and is clearly explained.

Student B

The researcher can be at least 95% certain that the difference in the mood scores was caused by the exercise and was not a chance effect.

@ **2/2 marks awarded.** Student B's answer is correct and is clearly explained.

12.6 The sport psychologist decided to submit the research to peer review. Explain why it is useful for psychological research to undergo peer review. (3 marks)

@ Question injunction = explain. This assesses AO3 skills and whether you understand at least one reason why peer review is useful.

Student A

Peers are professionals in the same field as the psychologist whose research is being reviewed. Peer reviews are useful because they can help to decide whether research is good enough to be published and positive peer reviews can catch the eye of journal editors. **a** Also, peer reviews are useful to university departments as positive peer reviews can improve the research credibility of a university/department. **b**

@ **3/3 marks awarded. a, b** Student A's answer is accurate and thorough and demonstrates a good understanding of the usefulness of peer review.

Student B

Peer reviews are useful because they decide whether research is good enough to be published. **a**

@ **1/3 marks awarded.** Student B's answer is only partially correct. The decision to publish research is made by a journal editor — peer review only influences the decision to publish.

12.7 When people contacted the sport psychologist he set up individual meetings in the sports club with the volunteer participants. In the meeting he briefed each participant about the research and what they would be asked to do.

Write a briefing that the sport psychologist could read out to each participant. (6 marks)

@ This question requires you to demonstrate AO1 and AO3 skills.

You should demonstrate knowledge of ethical guidelines, especially informed consent, no deception, protection of participants and the right to confidentiality. This question assesses whether you understand how important it is for psychologists to follow the ethical guidelines and to treat participants with care and respect.

Student A

Good morning. My name is Joel and I am very pleased to meet you. Thank you for coming to help my research. Before we start I will brief you on what you are going to be asked to do. The purpose of my research is to try to find out whether exercise has any effect on mood, specifically anxiousness and/or relaxation. a If you agree to participate I will first ask you to complete a short questionnaire in which you will be asked about how you are feeling now. Then I will take you to the running track and ask you to run 100 metres as fast as you can. b Please don't worry about this — if at any time you feel out of breath or just want to stop running you can. c After your run, I will ask you to complete another questionnaire which will also contain questions about how you feel. d Now that you know what you will be asked to do, if you would rather not participate that's fine, there is tea and coffee and soft drinks on the table at the side — please help yourself before you go home. e If you are still willing to participate you will not be asked to identify yourself in any way — your contribution to my research will be completely anonymous. f Before we start do you have any questions? g

e **6/6 marks awarded.** Student A has left nothing to chance — the briefing is clear, thorough and appropriate. a The student informs the participant about the true purpose of the study to gain informed consent. b The participant is told the truth about what they will be asked to do. c The participant is given the right to withdraw from running — which is important as their physical fitness to run is not being tested. d, e The participant is given the final information and reminded again that they don't have to participate — and by offering refreshments at this point the right to withdraw is made clear. f, g The participant is assured that their contribution will be anonymous and invited to ask questions. This is a well-written answer that demonstrates knowledge and understanding of the research process.

Student B

The purpose of the research is to find out whether exercise has any effect on mood. a I will first ask you to complete a short questionnaire in which you will be asked about how you are feeling. Then I will take you to the running track and ask you to run 100 metres. After your run, I will ask you to complete another questionnaire. b If you would rather not participate you have the right to withdraw. c If you want to carry on your contribution to my research will be completely anonymous. d

e **3–4/6 marks awarded.** Student B has written an appropriate briefing. a The student informs the participant about the true purpose of the study to gain informed consent. b The participant is told the truth about what they will be asked to do but is not reminded that they can stop running whenever they want to. c The participant is given the right to withdraw but this reminder is rather vague. d The participant is assured that their contribution will be anonymous. The answer demonstrates understanding of the ethical guidelines but could be developed more effectively.

Multiple-choice answers

Approaches in psychology

1.1 Correct answers:

C Behaviour is motivated by conscious mental processes.

B All behaviour is learned and can be unlearned.

D Behaviour is motivated by forces in the unconscious mind.

E Behaviour is motivated by the desire for self-actualisation and free will.

A Behaviour can be explained by studying the functions of physiological systems.

1.2 The answer is D. Cognitive behavioural therapy (CBT) is a talking cure in which patients like Anton are encouraged to examine their irrational thought processes and change the way they think about their experiences.

1.3 The answer is C. Congruence is a term used in humanistic psychology when a person's ideal self is consistent with what actually happens in the life and experiences of the person.

1.4 The answer is A. The loud noise is the unconditioned stimulus that normally causes a fear response. The white rat is the neutral stimulus that does not normally cause a fear response.

1.5 The answer is B. Self-actualisation (becoming all you can be) is a term associated with humanistic psychology.

Biopsychology

5.1 The correct answers are A, B and E. Sensory neurons carry messages in only one direction, are afferent neurons and receive information through dendrites of other neurons.

5.2 Correct answers:

C Serotonin: involved in mood, sleep and appetite and depression and anxiety disorders

D Endorphins: involved in pain relief and feelings of pleasure and contentedness

A Dopamine: correlated with movement, attention and learning

B Epinephrine: involved in energy and glucose metabolism

5.3 The answer is B. The flight or flight response originates in the sympathetic nervous system.

5.4 The answer is B. The brainstem is part of the brain but is not one of the four lobes.

5.5 The correct answers are A, B, D and E. An exogenous zeitgeber is an external pacemaker. Hormones are not exogenous pacemakers, they are endogenous (internal) pacemakers.

Research methods, scientific processes, data handling and inferential statistics

10.1 The answer is D. This is a field experiment.

10.2 The answer is C. It was an independent design. Each student was either in the desks in rows condition or the desks in a circle condition.

10.3 The answer is C. The IV is whether the desks are in rows or a circle.

10.4 The correct answers are B, C and E. Quantitative data; ordinal level data because scores range between 0 and 50; numerical data because scores on the test are numbers.

10.5 The correct answers are C and E. Covert observation because the students were unaware they were being observed; non-participant observation because the trainee teacher was not a member of the student group.

10.6 The answer is D. Opportunity sample — the participants were the students who just happened to be in the class with desks in rows or desks in a circle.

10.7 The correct answers are B and D. The mean scores and the median scores are both measures of central tendency.

10.8 The answer is C. Only the Mann-Whitney U test is appropriate for use in an independent design, where ordinal data are collected, and where a difference between conditions is being tested.

Knowledge check answers

1 The behaviourist approach assumes that all behaviour is learned in interaction with the environment; that what has been learned can be unlearned; that abnormal behaviour is learned in the same way as normal behaviour.

2 The neutral stimulus is the rat. The unconditioned stimulus is the loud noise.

3 Positive reinforcement is the pleasure we feel when our behaviour leads to pleasurable consequences. Negative reinforcement is the pleasure we feel when our behaviour stops something unpleasant from happening.

4 Possible areas include: memory, perception, language and decision making.

5 The cognitive approach is based on the assumption that the human mind is like an information processor and that people can control how they select, store and think about information; and that irrational beliefs are the cause of abnormality.

6 Genes, brain structure, biochemistry.

7 The biological approach assumes that there is a direct relationship between biology and behaviour and that behaviour has physical causes, for example, genes or neurotransmitters.

8 Adrenaline, dopamine, serotonin.

9 Oral, anal, phallic, latent, genital.

10 The psychodynamic approach assumes that the human personality has three parts, the id, ego and superego; that these three parts of the personality develop in five psychosexual stages and all behaviour is motivated by unconscious forces; and that abnormal behaviour has its origins in unresolved, unconscious conflicts in early childhood.

11 Self-actualisation is a process of growing and developing as a person in order to achieve maximum individual potential.

12 Humanistic psychologists recognise the existence of free will and assume that each person is a unique individual having a need for self-actualisation and the potential for personal growth. Another assumption is that if children receive unconditional positive regard they will develop satisfactorily. Humanistic psychologists rely on self-report methods, as they believe that how individuals report their own conscious experiences should be treated as evidence.

13 **Hierarchy of needs.** The escalating types of human needs, from the lower basic needs for food and shelter, for safety and security and for love and friendship, rising to the higher needs for personal growth and self-actualisation. **Unconditional positive regard** is where parents accept and love their child for what he or she is. **Congruence.** A person's ideal self is consistent with their self-image. **Incongruence.** There is a gap between a person's ideal self and their self-image.

14 **Reductionism.** Reducing complex human behaviour to simple single factor explanations, for example in psychology giving a biological explanation for behaviour and ignoring social or cognitive influences on behaviour. **Determinism.** Suggesting that human behaviour is caused by a factor outside our control (no human free will) such as genetic causes, unconscious forces, or past learning. The biological approach is reductionist and deterministic; the behavioural approach is reductionist and deterministic; the psychodynamic approach is deterministic.

15 The **central nervous system** comprises the brain and the spinal cord which act together. The spinal cord joins the brainstem which controls heartbeat, breathing, blood pressure, digestion as well as arousal and attention, sleep and wakefulness. The **peripheral nervous system** comprises the somatic nervous system to regulate the actions of the skeletal muscles and the autonomic nervous system which regulates primarily involuntary activity such as heart rate, breathing, blood pressure and digestion.

16 Neurons are only capable of carrying a message in one direction. Relay neurons relay information from sensory neurons to motor neurons bypassing the brain. Motor neurons are **efferent neurons** as they carry information from the brain to the target.

17 Dopamine — movement, attention and learning; serotonin — mood, sleep, appetite and aggression; epinephrine — energy and depression.

18 The **pituitary gland**, just beneath the hypothalamus, controls growth and regulates other glands. The **adrenal glands**, located at the top of each kidney, regulate moods, energy level, and the ability to cope with stress. The **pancreas**, located under the stomach, is a dual-purpose gland that performs both digestive and endocrine functions.

19 Findings include: (a) If a picture was first shown to the left visual field and then to the right visual field the participants did not recognise the picture as having been shown before. (b) If visual material appeared in the right visual field, the patient could describe it in speech and writing. (c) If visual material appeared to the left visual field the patient could identify the same object with their right hand but not their left hand.

20

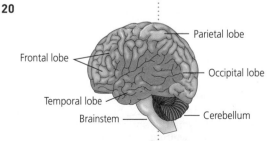

21 **Post-mortem studies** in which researchers conduct a study of the brain of an individual who may have had some sort of illness. **Electroencephalogram**

(EEG) which records the electrical activity and voltage fluctuations resulting from ionic current flows within the neurons of the brain. **Functional magnetic resonance imaging (fMRI)** is a procedure that uses MRI imaging to measure the metabolic changes that take place in an active part of the brain.

22 **Circadian rhythms:** cycles of behaviour that happen every 24 hours (around a day), for example sleeping/waking. **Infradian rhythms:** occur over a period of time greater than 24 hours, for example the menstrual cycle. **Ultradian rhythms:** repeat over a period of less than 24 hours, for example the stages of sleep.

23 In NREM sleep brain activity is synchronised, brain waves become higher in amplitude, and the body is very relaxed, heart rate and blood pressure fall. In REM sleep brain activity is desynchronised, the brain becomes very active and heart rate and blood pressure increase and the eyes move rapidly giving this stage its name.

24 This is a laboratory experiment using standardised procedures — all students had 1 minute to memorise the same list of words and then 1 minute to write down as many as they could remember.

25 This is a (quasi) natural experiment. The IV is whether the child had been in day nursery or looked after by a child minder and this IV is naturally occurring — you cannot randomly allocate children to be looked after by a nursery or child minder.

26 **Naturalistic observation** where people are observed in their natural environment without any manipulation of variables and without their knowledge. **Controlled observation** where the researcher manipulates the behaviour of the observers or the observed. **Overt observation** in which participants know they are being observed. This reduces ethical issues of consent and privacy but reduces validity due to increased demand characteristics. **Participant observation** where the researchers get involved with the group of participants they are observing.

27 Is your child smiling and happy to see you at the end of the day in childcare? YES or NO

28 This would suggest there is a positive relationship between the number of hours spent revising and performance in a psychology test — as hours revising increase so do test scores.

29 Qualitative data.

30 Debriefing is carried out after participants have carried out the study.

31 Possible ethical issues include: gaining informed consent; protecting participants from harm by ensuring they were not asked embarrassing questions about parents or their relationships.

32 That the strength of the verb used in the leading question (contacted, bumped, hit, collided, smashed) will have no effect on the speed the participants report the cars travelling.

33 That there are significantly more reports of seeing broken glass from participants who were asked 'how fast the cars were travelling when they smashed into each other' than from participants who were asked 'how fast the cars were travelling when they hit each other'.

34 An opportunity sample is usually a sample of people approached by the researcher in one area or location and as such is always culturally biased.

35 To select a systematic sample of 20 psychology students you will pick every 10th name from the list of 200 names.

36 In an independent design each participant only experiences one of the experimental conditions. In a repeated measures design each participant experiences all the experimental conditions.

37 Using the phone to send text messages; using the phone to take photographs; using the phone to speak to someone.

38 Qualitative data.

39 Operationalisation means making variables measurable by clearly defining them. For example, Milgram operationalised obedience as the highest level of electric shock voltage his participants administered to Mr Wallace before they refused to continue.

40 Aggressive behaviour in children is socially undesirable, so because parents would want people to approve of their children they would be less likely to answer that their child behaves aggressively very often or often.

41 Peer reviews are useful to: (a) help to determine where research funding should go; (b) help decide whether research is good enough to be published; (c) improve the research rating and credibility of a university/department.

42 The internal validity of an experiment may be reduced by uncontrolled extraneous variables; by demand characteristics; by not using standardised procedures.

43 Because psychology has several different approaches to explaining human behaviour (cognitive, behaviourist, biological, psychodynamic, humanistic) Kuhn would argue that psychologists do not have universal laws of human behaviour (one paradigm) and thus that psychology cannot be a science.

44 Abstract; Introduction; Method; Results; Discussion; References.

45 A disadvantage of the mean as a measure of central tendency is that, especially in small data samples, it can be distorted by extremely high or low scores.

46 A measure of central tendency tells us the central point of a set of scores, a measure of dispersion tells us how the scores are spread out.

47 Possible categories include: healthy, protective, preventative, pleasurable, erotic.

48 Repeated measures — it looks at the direction of difference between two sets of scores from the same participants.

49 $P = < 0.05$ means that the probably of the result occurring by chance is equal to or less than 5%.

Note: **Bold** page numbers indicate glossary definitions.

Index